Pagan Portals – By Wolfsbane and Mandrake Root

The dark side of me lo  suspect I'm not alone in this. The F gets a lot of visitors each year in te mes furtive, interest. Draco's book i ancient arte and history of poisons, which goes back certainly beyond 4,500 years and probably throughout human history. I like Draco's writing style, which is both authoritative and accessible, I feel as if she's talking with me over a cup of tea and I really like that. After the history there's a fascinating chapter on 'The Proving Tree', about both cooking up and neutralizing poisons, including magical methods. It reminds me of Sir George Ripley the 15th century Yorkshire alchemist, a favourite of mine. Then there's a very useful chapter on the plants followed by a fascinating one on cursing and bottling, with reminders that you're responsible for everything you do! And a short but useful bibliography. Altogether an excellent little book. Thoroughly recommended.

Elen Sentier, shaman and author of *Shaman Pathways – Elen of the Ways*

Mélusine Draco has written a fascinating book that, despite being very small, manages to cover a tremendous amount of ground. It really brought home to me the way in which medicinal plants, used badly, can result in poisonous outcomes. The old adage that to be able to heal you have to be able to hex certainly holds true, because if you don't know what will prove lethal your chances of working safely are much reduced. Full of history, myths, plant details and sensible advice, this is a must-have book, and a great antidote to the poisonous idea that anything natural must be good.

Nimue Brown, Druid and author of *Druidry and the Ancestors*

Pagan Portals

By Wolfsbane and Mandrake Root

The Shadow World of Plants and their Poisons

Pagan Portals

By Wolfsbane and Mandrake Root

The Shadow World of Plants and their Poisons

Mélusine Draco

MOON
BOOKS

Winchester, UK
Washington, USA

First published by Moon Books, 2017
Moon Books is an imprint of John Hunt Publishing Ltd., Laurel House, Station Approach,
Alresford, Hants, SO24 9JH, UK
office1@jhpbooks.net
www.johnhuntpublishing.com
www.moon-books.net

For distributor details and how to order please visit the 'Ordering' section on our website.

Text copyright: Mélusine Draco 2016

ISBN: 978 1 78099 572 4
978 1 78099 628 8 (ebook)
Library of Congress Control Number: 2016949319

A CIP catalogue record for this book is available from the British Library.

Design: Stuart Davies

Printed and bound by CPI Group (UK) Ltd, Croydon, CR0 4YY, UK

Disclaimer: Natural poisons have been an integral ingredient
of traditional witchcraft for centuries and the information
contained within the text of *Pagan Portals – By Wolfsbane and
Mandrake Root* is for interest only. Neither the author nor
the publisher are responsible for the inappropriate,
unprofessional, criminal or ill-fated misuse of such plants. Let
the wise reader learn and the fool beware.

We operate a distinctive and ethical publishing philosophy in all
areas of our business, from our global network of authors to
production and worldwide distribution.

CONTENTS

About the Author   viii

Introduction   1

Chapter One: A Touch of Poison   5

Chapter Two: The Proving Tree   23

Chapter Three: Poisonous Flora   31

Chapter Four: Cursing v Bottling   71

Afterthought   81

Sources & Bibliography   83

About the Author

Mélusine Draco's highly individualistic teaching methods and writing draw on historical sources supported by academic texts and current archaeological findings; endorsing the view that magic is an amalgam of science and art, and that magic is the outer route to the inner Mysteries. She is the author of several titles currently published with John Hunt Publishing including the best-selling six-part Traditional Witchcraft series; two titles on power animals – *Aubry's Dog* and *Black Horse, White Horse; By Spellbook & Candle: Cursing, Hexing, Bottling and Binding; The Secret People; Pan: Dark Lord of the Forest; The Dictionary of Magic & Mystery* published by Moon Books; *Magic Crystals Sacred Stones* and *The Atum-Re Revival* published by Axis Mundi Books. She is also Principal of Coven of the Scales and the Temple of Khem.

Links

Website:
www.covenofthescales.com
Website:
www.templeofkhem.com
Blog:
melusinedracoattempleofkhem.blogspot.com/
Facebook:
www.facebook.com/Melusine-Draco-486677478165958
Facebook:
www.facebook.com/TradBritOldCraft
Facebook:
www.facebook.com/TempleofKhem
Facebook:
www.facebook.com/TempleHouseArchive

Introduction

The crime of poisoning, or 'veneficium', according to the *JM Latin-English Dictionary*, involves magic and sorcery, the mixing of poison and the administering of poisoned drinks by a *veneficus* (male sorcerer) or *venefica* (female sorceress) as defined by such classic writers as Ovid, Pliny, Cicero and Horace. The art of poisoning, however, goes back to the dawn of time when humans first discovered the *Solanaceae* genus of plants and learned of their great powers – and their dangers. Those who knew these secrets later became greatly feared and/or respected in their communities and the knowledge passed into the province of witchcraft and shamanism.

Daniel A Schulke's now highly collectable *Veneficium: Magic, Witchcraft and the Poison Path* offered a valuable insight into this intersection of magic and poison that originated in remotest antiquity and reaches into the present day. Pointing out that beyond their functions as agents of bodily harm, poisons have also served as gateways of religious ecstasy, occult knowledge, and sensorial aberration, as well as the basis of many cures, he wrote: 'Allied with Samael, the Edenic serpent of first transgression whose name in some interpretations is 'Venom of God', this facet of magic wends through the rites of ancient Sumer and Egypt, through European necromancy, alchemy, the arcane the rites of the Witches' Sabbath, and modern-day folk magic.'

Slowly we begin to realise that the knowledge and use of poison within witchcraft goes beyond the consideration of its 'toxicological dimensions of magical power', as Schulke examines the 'concurrent thread of astral and philosophical poisons ... and explores 'their resonance and dissonance with magical practice'. He included in his study the herbs of the so-called 'Devil's Garden', in context with the witches' supper, and the *Unguentum Sabbati*, the much-written about flying ointment that has exerted its fascination over scholar, historian, and magical practitioner alike.

Nevertheless, poisoning has always had a close connection with witchcraft and the powers of sorcery. Ever since the mis-transliteration of biblical texts replaced the original, 'Thou shalt not suffer a *poisoner* to live', with, 'Thou shalt not suffer a *witch* to live', the two have remained synonymous even unto the present day. The introduction of laws against witchcraft and the rise of the witch-mania in Europe condemned simple village wise-women, herbalists and midwives to constant accusations of being poisoners, abortionists and witches. In reality their knowledge of botanical medicines was probably far superior to that of the newly emerging breed of physicians, who did not study the subject scientifically until the end of the 16th century.

The wise-woman who was equipped with the means and knowledge to kill as well as cure, was extremely vulnerable when death occurred under what was seen as 'mysterious circum-stances'. Eric Maple in *Man, Myth & Magic* says that there is some evidence to suggest that this new medical profession had a vested interest in branding its rivals as poisoners and witches in order to rid itself of the competition. Especially, because of the deficiencies of the physicians of the time, these wise-women were in constant demand for the treatment of the sick and the poor.

The pharmacopoeia of witchcraft incorporated the common run of botanical recipes from woodland and hedgerow which were readily available to anyone with murder or abortion in mind. ... the most notorious poisons being hemlock, hemp and henbane. In unskilful hands an aphrodisiac like cantharides could cause agonising death. Among the more general types of abortifacients were the potentially poisonous pennyroyal, rye ergot and oil of tansy ...

Not surprisingly, the physicians took every opportunity to cast blame for their failures on their rival – witchcraft – which was backed up by Church sanctions, since Inquisitional doctrine decreed that all diseases beyond the curative power of medicine must be due to sorcery! During the late 16th and early 17th centuries, however, it was still beyond the capacity of most physicians to determine what was or was not a poisonous substance. During the witchcraft hysteria, when all forms of magical healing were stigmatised as heresy, it is easy to see why the healing virtues of the local wise-woman were viewed as 'veneficium' rather than the practise of genuine domestic plant medicine, should anything go wrong.

Strangely to our modern way of thinking, poisoning has always been referred to as an 'arte', possibly because its association can be found in the Greek word *pharmakos*, used to refer to herbal remedies, spell-potions and poisons – and those who crafted them. The association with witchcraft was also echoed in Charles G Leland's inflammatory translation of *Aradia, or the Gospel of the Witches* (1899) with the words:

And thou shalt be the first of witches known;
And thou shalt be the first of all in the world:
And thou shalt teach the art of poisoning,
Of poisoning those who are great Lords of all;
Yea, thou shalt make them die in their palaces ...

Compiled by American folklorist Charles Godfrey Leland, *Aradia* contained what was purported to be a genuine glimpse into the world of Tuscan witchcraft, although scholars are still divided; some dismissing Leland's assertion regarding the origins of the manuscript, and others arguing for its authenticity as a unique documentation of folk beliefs. Nevertheless, the text firmly endorses Italian witches as being practitioners of 'veneficium'.

In all honesty, witch-lore *is* closely tied to a knowledge of poisonous plants as part of its folk-medicine, simply because it is necessary to know what can kill or cure (in either large or small doses) as part of the oral training; and a wide familiarity with *all* wild plants is an essential skill within traditional witchcraft. Some plants have beneficial components while others can be lethal if the wrong treatment is given – and as it's suggested in *Veneficium: Magic, Witchcraft and the Poison Path*, poisonous plants can also be utilised as powerful magical ingredients in Circle whenever necessary.

Chapter One

A Touch of Poison

The history of poison has a long pedigree that stretches back to before 4500BC with one of the most famous cases of poisoning being the sentence passed on Socrates (399BC), who drank hemlock having been found guilty of neglecting the officially accepted gods and corrupting the minds of the youth of Athens. Socrates' death is described at the end of Plato's *Phaedo*:

> After drinking the poison, he was instructed to walk around until his legs felt numb. After he lay down, the man who administered the poison pinched his foot; Socrates could no longer feel his legs. The numbness slowly crept up his body until it reached his heart. Shortly before his death, Socrates speaks his last words to his friend Crito: '*Crito, we owe a rooster to Asclepius. Please, don't forget to pay the debt.*'

In Greek mythology, when Jason left the sorceress Medea to marry Glauce, Medea took her revenge by sending Glauce a poison dress and a golden coronet, also dipped in poison. This resulted in the death of the princess and, subsequently, her father, when he tried to save her. The 'Shirt of Nessus' refers to the garment smeared with the poisoned blood of the centaur Nessus, which was given to Hercules by his wife, Deianira. Deianira had been tricked by Nessus into believing that his blood would ensure that Hercules would remain faithful. According to Sophocles' tragedy *The Women of Trachis*, Hercules began to perspire when he donned the shirt, which soon clung to his flesh, corroding it. He eventually threw himself onto a pyre in extreme agony and was burnt to death. Sophocles' play *Trachinia* is extensively based on a retelling of this myth.

Poison arrows were actually used by real peoples in the ancient world, including the Gauls, Romans, and the Scythians; with Greek and Roman historians describing recipes for poisoning projectiles and citing historical battles in which poison arrows were used. Alexander the Great encountered poisoned projectiles during his conquest of India (possibly dipped in the venom of Russell's viper), and the army of the Roman general Lucullus suffered grievous poison wounds from arrows shot by nomads during the Third Mithridatic War (1st century BC).

According to the BBC's *Shakespeare Lives: Poisons, Potions and Drugs*, poisoned potions were also the weapons of choice for many of Shakespeare's most iconic characters; used to seduce lovers, kill enemies and gain power, nothing was too lethal for the Bard. Poison takes a leading role in *Hamlet*, as sibling rivalry leads to regicide and throws the Danish royal castle at Elsinore into a state of jealously and murder. The Danish king, father to Hamlet and brother to Claudius, dies seemingly in his sleep, but his son soon discovers via a ghostly visitation from his deceased father that poison in the ear was in fact the cause: *'With juice of cursed hebenon in a vial; And in the porches of my ears did pour.'* Scientists and scholars have wondered what Shakespeare meant by 'cursed hebenon' and there may be a few possibilities including hemlock, nightshade, yew, ebony and henbane. Indeed henbane looks the closest in spelling, and the active ingredient in henbane is hyoscyamine, which if concentrated to a high degree could be lethal to humans.

In the final act of *Romeo and Juliet*, our tragic heroine takes a potion to fake her own death and place her into a catatonic state – and many believe the potion is most likely to be deadly nightshade (*atropa belladonna*). Upon finding Juliet and believing her to be dead, Romeo uses a powerful, fast-acting poison to take his own life; an obvious choice for such a strong poison is potassium cyanide or the medieval monkshood, both of which cause rapid respiratory failure. *'Put this in any liquid thing you will, and drink it off; and, if you had the strength of twenty men, it would dispatch you straight.'*

In *Antony and Cleopatra*, the Queen on learning of Mark Antony's death and being unwilling to be taken alive by Caesar, sets in motion her own suicide by an asp bite to the breast. Most ancient sources say that the snake was smuggled into her room in a basket of figs and Plutarch wrote that she performed experiments on condemned prisoners and found 'aspis' venom to be the most painless of all fatal poisons. This 'aspis' was far more likely to be *Naja haje* (the Egyptian cobra noted for its particularly bad temper) than any other type of snake since a stylised image in the form of the uraeus representing the goddess Wadjet was the symbol of sovereignty for the Pharaohs who incorporated its image into their diadem. This iconography was continued through the Ptolemaic Kingdom. The venom that was most likely used by Cleopatra was both neurotoxic and cytotoxic and would have caused a particularly excruciating death; the venom first stops signals to the muscles and later to the heart and lungs – victims die from respiratory failure.

In *Macbeth*, the three witches brew a potion with ingredients chosen to symbolise incredible evil. Amongst human organs and animal parts, the witches use the root of the deadly hemlock (*conium maculatum*), a highly poisonous plant known to have a chemical structure and pharmacological properties similar to nicotine. Even in low doses, the plant can cause respiratory failure and death. The root of the plant used by the witches in their deadly concoction is known to have the highest toxicity concentration of all of the plant. They also added yew (*taxus baccata*), which contains the highly toxic alkaloid taxine, which if ingested can cause rapid death through cardiac arrest. It is also significant that the witches were boiling their broth, since boiling has long been known to sterilise water and destroy pathogenic, disease causing micro-organisms. The increased temperature would also give the molecules more kinetic energy and the reaction would proceed faster. The scene is one of the most evocative in all of Shakespeare's works and has inspired many writers from J K Rowling to Samuel Beckett. Though the fictional potion is a magical creation, the deathly potential of the ingredients used is very real, since the plants are some of the most poisonous species found in western Europe and it is evident that Shakespeare was aware of their lethal nature.

Less lethal, one of the most famous love potions is administered by Puck in *A Midsummer Night's Dream*, and made from a flower called 'love-in-idleness', otherwise known as the wild pansy (*viola tricola*). The potion was created when Cupid shoots an arrow at 'the imperial votaress', but misses and instead hits the flower. The petals turn from white to purple, and the flower's juice becomes a love potion. Puck then places the potion on the sleeping eyes of Lysander, and later Demetrius, which causes chaos in the forest.

It was during the Roman Empire, however, that poisoning became one of the more prevalent means of assassination. As early as 331BC, poisonings executed at the dinner table or in drinks were reported, and the practice became a common occurrence. The use of fatal substances was seen among every social class; even the nobility would often use it to dispose of unwanted political or economic opponents.

According to Robert Graves' novel *I, Claudius*, Livia – wife of Augustus – managed to poison anyone who threatened the stability of the Empire; but there were also contemporary rumours mentioned by Tacitus and Cassius Dio that Livia had brought about Augustus's death by poisoning fresh figs. The writer Livy describes the poisoning of members of the upper class and nobles of Rome, and the Roman Emperor Nero is known to have favoured the use of poisons on his relatives, even hiring a personal poisoner. His preferred poison was said to be cyanide. Nero's predecessor, Claudius, was also allegedly poisoned with mushrooms by his wife Agrippina because she was ambitious for her son, Nero, and Claudius had become suspicious of her intrigues

Mithridates VI, King of Pontus (114BC-63BC), lived in constant fear of being assassinated through poison and became a pioneer in the search for antidotes. In his position of power, he was able to test poisons on criminals facing execution, and then experiment to see if there was a possible antidote. Paranoid to the point of administering daily amounts of poisons in an attempt to make himself immune to as many poisons as he could, he eventually discovered a formula that combined small portions of dozens of the best-known herbal remedies of the time, which he named Mithridatium.

After being defeated by Pompey the Great, Mithridates' antidote prescriptions and notes of medicinal plants were taken by the Romans and translated into Latin. He had invented a complex 'universal antidote' against poisoning; Aulus Cornelius Celsus gives one version in his *De Medicina* and names it *Antidotum Mithridaticum*. Pliny the Elder's version comprised 54 ingredients to be placed in a flask and matured for at least two months. In keeping with most medical practices of the time, Mithridates' anti-poison routines and formula included a religious component that was supervised by the *Agari*, a group of Scythian shamans who never left him. Pliny the Elder describes more than 7,000 different poisons; one being: 'The blood of a duck found in a certain district of Pontus, which was supposed to live on poisonous food, and the blood of this duck was afterwards used in the preparation of the Mithridatum, because it fed on poisonous plants and suffered no harm.'

In medieval Europe, poison became an even more popular form of killing, though antidotes surfaced for many of the more widely known toxins. The preference for this kind of murder was stimulated by the increased availability of poisons; shops known as apothecaries were selling various medicinal products and from there, substances that were traditionally used for healing were often utilised for more sinister ends. In the Middle East, around the same time, a form of arsenic was developed that was odourless and transparent, making the poison difficult to detect. This 'poison epidemic' was a means widely employed by both rich and poor to get rid of unwanted rivals and annoying members of the family.

The House of Borgia became prominent in ecclesiastical and political affairs in the 15th and 16th centuries, producing two popes: Alfons de Borja (Pope Callixtus III) and Rodrigo Lanzol Borgia (Pope Alexander VI). As a family they were suspected of many crimes, including incest and murder, especially murder by arsenic poisoning and the most widely accused were Pope Alexander VI, and his son, Cesare. Some claim that arsenic actually improved the taste of wine, but whether true or not, the Borgias made certain that their guest consumed as much of the doctored drink as possible. Following the inevitable and untimely death of the victim, ownership of his property – by Church law – reverted to the Borgias.

On an occasion when some cardinals were scheduled later in the evening to receive the Borgia's hospitality, the Pope and Cesare returned home early and called for a bottle of wine in premature celebration. Whether by accident or design, a servant brought the wrong bottle. The Pope died, but Cesare, after having a mule slaughtered and dressed, wrapped the carcass about himself in accord with the ancient superstition that entering the body of an animal warded off the effects of poisons. His recovery seems to be the only known proof that such a remedy actually works, but he was never again to be in a position of wealth and power.

The origin of the expression 'the gift of the Borgias' is obscure, but it might have reflected the sarcastic wit of some unknown historian. It may be relevant that the German word 'gift' means both poison and malice.

The House of Medici was an Italian banking family, political dynasty and later royal house that first began to gather prominence during the first half of the 15th century. The family produced three popes: Pope Leo X; Pope Clement VII and Pope Leo XI; two regent queens of France: Catherine de' Medici and Marie de' Medici and hereditary Dukes of Florence.

The massive Chateau de Blois has been home to many notable members of the French aristocracy, but none more notorious than the murderous Medici clan. Catherine de' Medici, wife to one French king and mother to three more, died at Blois in 1589. She was the original evil stepmother, ultimate meddler in the affairs of her children and therefore matters of State, and notorious for the mysterious yet convenient deaths of her enemies. For generations, the room full of tiny cabinets at the famous chateau has been described to visitors as Catherine de' Medici's private apothecary and cabinet of horrors, home to her extensive collection of deadly poisons.

The room in question holds 237 small cabinets, hidden in the beautiful woodwork. The room was associated with Catherine de' Medici, and she was certainly suspected of some heinous poison-related crimes, but historians cannot confirm that the legend is true. The chateau is also the site of the elaborate assassination of the Duke of Guise, plotted by Henry III (third son of Catherine). It is worth mentioning that at the time, Italians in general, and women in particular, were widely suspected of being poisoners. Catherine definitely ordered the killing of a handful of people, but whether she dispatched them herself by poison is questionable.

'Thou mixture rank, of midnight weeds collected, with Hecate's ban thrice blasted, thrice infected ...' comes from the 'play' scene from Shakespeare's *Hamlet* and shows how popular the poison theme was with the theatre crowd back in the 16th century. The principal target of the poisoner's art, however, has always been the

husband or wife who had outlived their desirability and usefulness, the heir who stood between the poisoner and an inheritance, or the removal of a rival. Women, it seems, were the main offenders, as Reginald Scot makes clear in his *Discovery of Witchcraft* (1584), in which he declared 'women to have been the first inventors of poisoning and more naturally addicted thereunto than men' – thereby taking a side-swipe at the botanical skills of the local wise-women.

Chambre Ardente Affaire

The most infamous and far-reaching case involving poisoning and witchcraft, however, was the *Chambre Ardente Affaire*, with its black masses and 'Catholic priests gashing newborn babies over the breasts of naked girls stretched out over altars', according to Professor Rossell Hope Robbins in *The Encyclopaedia of Witchcraft and Demonology*. This was probably the *only* 'witch' trial ever based on some element of truth, rather than on the wild imaginings of young neurotics or the morbid logic of perverse judges and Inquisitors. The investigation called witnesses before the *Chambre Ardente* – so-called because the room was draped in black and lit with candles – a Star Chamber set up by Louis XIV to enquire into the widespread poisoning among the French nobility.

In the fictional style of Dennis Wheatley, the *Chambre Ardente Affaire* brought rumours of the 'Black Mass' to public attention for the first time, painting lurid pictures of frenzied priests sprinkling the breast of naked girls with fresh blood. The *Affaire* really did have all the trappings of a best-selling novel and involved an international poison-ring, royal ladies-in-waiting, a favourite of the King, one of his mistresses, the Captain of the King's Guard, and two rather unwholesome, money-grabbing characters, namely La Boss and La Voisin who were subsequently burned as a result of their involvement in this *cause célebre*.

Suggestions of Satanism and witchcraft had already crept into the sweeping accusations of poisoning, and under torture came confessions admitting to the sacrifice of children and white doves, and one admission of practising 'abominations with a big Easter candle'. A succession of unsavoury characters related an ever-increasing catalogue of equally unsavoury stories until the whole *Affaire* began to get completely out of hand. The biggest problem that faced the investigating officers was the difficulty of stifling the most humiliating scandal of the century. In 1709, Louis decided to destroy the records, but fortunately for posterity, the police commissioner's notes escaped destruction.

The original investigations (1673) had grown out of two prominent clergymen of the Notre Dame reporting to the police that most of their penitents confessed to either attempted or actual murder by poison! Eventually a well-established international poison supply-chain was uncovered, with connections in Portugal, Italy and England, that distributed poisons throughout France; huge stores of poison were discovered and some several hundred courtiers were implicated.

Ironically, despite the seriousness of the accusations, no members of the nobility were executed, and the principal villains of the piece, La Boss and La Voisin, both were generally thought of as fortune-tellers and abortionists for their classy clientele who provided poison on the side, rather than genuine witches. To this point, according to Professor Robbins, witchcraft was not involved; sorcery, yes – since the fortune-tellers sold love philtres (*poudres pour l'amour*) – and neither did witchcraft figure in the evidence collected later from other fortune-tellers.

The Medieval and Renaissance Poisoner

Similarly, the later English witch trials produced several accusations of poisoning, but it never played an important role, despite the *Maleficia* claiming that witches poisoned people with deadly concoctions and killing ointments at every turn.

The poisons used by witches are compounded and mixed from many sorts of poisons, such as the leaves and stalks and roots of plants; from animals, fishes and venomous reptiles, stones and metals; sometimes these are reduced to powder and sometimes to an ointment. It must also be known that witches administer such poisons either by causing them to be swallowed, or by external application. In the first instance they usually mix some poisonous powder with the food or drink; in the second they bewitch their victim, whether man or woman, while he is sleeping by anointing him with their lotions, waters, oils and unguents which contain many and various poisons. They anoint the thighs, or belly, or head, throat, breasts, ribs or some other part of the body of the person to be bewitched, who being asleep feels nothing; but such is the potency of that unguent that, as it is slowly absorbed by the heat of the sleeper's body, it enters his flesh and penetrates his vitals, causing his the greatest bodily pain ...

[Guazzo *Compendium Maleficarum*]

Scattered laws against witchcraft had been made in England from very early times, but the penalties were not severe; although under Athelstan (925AD-39AD) death was the penalty for murder by means of witchcraft. A woman found guilty of poisoning her husband was liable to suffer death at the stake for the crime of petit-treason. In 1652 the diarist John Evelyn witnessed the burning alive of a woman sentenced for husband murder, on a blazing tar barrel at Smithfield before a vast crowd – but not for practising witchcraft.

Other formulas for deadly poisons of the time were recorded by one Johann Weyer, a Dutch physician, occultist and demonologist, disciple and follower of Cornelius Agrippa, who later became court doctor to the Duke of Cleves:

- Hemlock, juice of aconite, poplar leaves and soot
- Water hemlock, sweet flag, cinquefoil, bat's blood, belladonna, oil
- Baby's fat, juice of water hemlock, aconite, cinquefoil, belladonna and soot

Some of these ingredients also appear in the infamous recipes for witches' flying ointment. It is known how some of these preparations were made because a number of English and Continental writers in the 16th and 17th centuries described the methods. All the recipes contained extracts from such strongly poisonous plants such as aconite, deadly nightshade and hemlock, together with cinquefoil, sweet flag, poplar leaves and parsley, mixed with soot and some sort of binding oil.

Generally speaking, the poisons had an arsenic base, which in acid form was tasteless and undetectable in the corpse. In addition, the professional poisoners used red and yellow sulphur, vitriol, all mixed with various other disgusting ingredients such as bat's blood, toad's venom, various toxic plants and bodily secretions for added potency! In truth, a medieval poisoner had a variety of choices: deadly herbs (henbane), toxic mushrooms (death angel) and other deadly foodstuffs, animal venom or fluids (snake venom, rabid dog saliva), heavy metals and minerals (such as mercury), and other plant-derived poisons (ergot fungus growing on rye and other grains). Terence Scully, a noted medieval food historian, has written several books on English and French Middle Ages cooking which support this fact, including *The Art of Cooking in the Middle Ages*:

In actual fact a person intent upon poisoning another person in the Middle Ages had a good variety of poisons at hand to draw upon – what we might well consider an *embarras de choix*. There was the very common poison obtained from monkshood or wolfsbane; hemlock, the umbelliferous plant (not, of course, the variety of spruce), yielded just as potent a poison as in Socrates' day; black hyoscyamus from the herb henbane, could be relied upon by any poisoner, as could thorn apple; and those dear old stand-bys, arsenic, mercury, and antimony sulfide could be sprinkled, or diluted, or spread with dependably efficacious results. It was quite understandable if the sundry resources that were available to the potential poisoner might make the object of his plotting somewhat anxious.

The great triumvirate of medieval plant poisons was belladonna, monkshood/wolfsbane, and foxglove. Interestingly enough, not only were they commonly used as poisons, but were also listed in nearly every witch's 'flying ointment' recipe – probably because of the hallucinogenic properties of such a combination. Belladonna, a paralytic, causes people to fall asleep – usually permanently. The ancient world believed that wolfsbane would cure belladonna poisoning and *vice versa*, but this has never been proven. On the other hand, belladonna (or more specifically atropine, which is derived from belladonna) is a modern cure for foxglove poisoning; and atropine being the antidote to monkshood is no folklore since digitalis, the modern heart medication now derived from foxglove, is a treatment for monkshood, or aconite poisoning.

Veneficium and Petit-Treason

From all the propaganda surrounding poisons throughout the ages, however, it is obvious that it was not necessarily the province of the witch when it came to disposing of problem people. In fact, it is evident that far more so-called 'respectable' folk were privy to the uses and effects of poison than ever died on scaffold or pyre in the name of witchcraft. Even in more modern times, including the 20th century, there were still those willing to utilise this ancient form of murder – for the same old reasons – on their way to an appointment with the executioner.

It is important to understand the implications of the charge of petit treason (murder of a husband by his wife, or a master by a servant, or a religious superior by a religious inferior) under English law for married women charged with murdering their husbands. From 1351-1828, a woman accused of killing her husband was liable to be indicted not for wilful murder, but for the aggravated offense of petit treason and, until 1790, she faced public execution by burning if convicted. In the legal paper *Petit Treason in 18th century England: Women's Inequality Before the Law*, Shelley A McGavigan outlined the legal aspects behind the Law of Petit Treason, which became a statutory offence during the reign of Edward III. The Statute of Treasons distinguished between two types:

> High treason is declared to be the offence against the king; petit treason the offence against the lord – thus preserving an interesting survival of the old Anglo-Saxon idea that treason is a form of treachery. At common law, 'murders of a particular class were separated from other cases of homicide by being classified as petty [sic] treason ...'

By the end of the 13th century, several offences against either one's lord or one's king were first codified as being treasonable during King Edward III's reign by the Treason Act 1351. It clarified exactly what crimes constituted treason, following earlier, somewhat 'over zealous' interpretations of England's legal codes. For instance, high treason could be committed by anyone found to be compassing (forecasting) the king's death, or counterfeiting his coin, and remained distinct from what became known as petit treason. Though 12th century contemporary authors made few attempts to differentiate between high treason and petty treason, enhanced punishments indicate that the latter was treated more seriously than ordinary felony. In England, burning was a legal punishment inflicted on women found guilty of high treason, petty treason and heresy. Over a period of several centuries, women were publicly burnt at the stake, sometimes alive, for a range of other activities including coining, mariticide and poisoning.

English law of 1531 allowed poisoners to be boiled alive, and in 1532 a cook called Richard Roose (or Rouse) suffered this fate. Roose was a cook to John Fisher, bishop of Rochester, who was executed for attempting to poison Fisher and was the first person in England executed by being boiled to death. According to one of Fisher's earliest biographers, one Richard Hall, Roose came into the Bishop's kitchen and put poison into the gruel that was being prepared for the Bishop's dinner. Fortunately for the Bishop, he had no appetite and instead his guests and servants ate the poisoned meal. *'One gentleman, named Mr. Bennet Curwen and an old widow, died suddenly, and the rest never recovered their health till their dying day.'* Roose was apprehended and admitted to adding what he believed were laxatives to the meal as a jest – but no one was laughing.

Inexplicably, Henry VIII decided that Roose should be condemned by attainder without a trial, which was an unusual measure – even for Henry – since attainder was used for criminals who were at large and Roose had been already arrested. The Parliament of England passed 'An Acte for Poysoning', making wilful murder by means of poison high treason, even if the victim was not the head of the government of the land, and boiling to death became the punishment for this crime.

Ambassador Eustace Chapuys wrote a slightly different version of the story to his master, Charles V, the nephew of Catherine of Aragon:

They say that the cook, having been immediately arrested... confessed at once that he had actually put into the broth some powders, which he had been given to understand would only make his fellow servants very sick without endangering their lives or doing them any harm. I have not yet been able to understand who it was who gave the cook such advice, nor for what purpose.

Like the later *Chambre Ardente Affaire* there was probably a royal scandal in the offing, since Bishop Fisher was Catherine of Aragon's most staunch defender over her impending divorce from Henry VIII. History does not record who put the unfortunate Roose up to poisoning the Bishop's dinner, but the swiftness of his disposal strongly hints at another conspiracy at court!

In the *Chronicle of the Grey Friars of London* (1852), a history of London from the late 12th to the mid-16th century, a poisoner is said to have met his death by being lowered on a chain into boiling water at Smithfield in 1522. However, the only extant legislative notice of boiling in England occurred in the Act passed in 1531 during the reign of Henry VIII, the preamble of which made poisoning a form of petit treason. The statute named Richard Rouse who, *'by putting poisoned yeast in porridge prepared for the household of the Bishop of Rochester and the poor of Lambeth parish, sickened 17 people and killed a man and a woman.'* He was found guilty of petty treason and publicly boiled at Smithfield. Some months later a maidservant was boiled at King's Lynn for poisoning her mistress, and in 1542 Margaret Davy or Dawes, a servant, was boiled at Smithfield for poisoning her employer. The law was repealed in 1547.

A pamphlet detailing the burning at Tyburn in April 1652 of Joan Peterson, the so-called Witch of Wapping, served to bring for the first time, accusations of both witchcraft *and* poisoning into the equation. When an elderly Lady Powell died, leaving her wealth to a particular relative, much to the chagrin of other interested parties, they contrived to have Anne Livingston charged with 'witchery' in order to separate her from her windfall and get their own hands on the bequest.

When Joan Peterson, a local healer with a knack for fixing migraines, refused a bribe to accuse Anne Livingston of sorcering [sic], the plotters made it an offer she couldn't refuse (and protected themselves from exposure) by accusing Joan herself. But they weren't targeting Joan Peterson at all. They just wanted to use her to get at Livingston. Our pamphlet presents a riveting and revolting story of the conspirators essentially being one with the local judicial officials – in fact, when it comes to trial, they're literally Joan Peterson's judges – *'but even as they groped her for witches' teats and the like, they endeavoured to persuade the said Peterson to confess [since] she needed not fear what she confessed, for it was not her life they aimed at, but to have matter whereby to accuse one Mrs. Levingston [sic], who had gotten the said Lady Powels estate, and thereby had undone 36 Persons of the said Ladyes Kindred.'*

According to Shelley McGavigan:

Because poison, women and murder seem to have been inextricably entwined throughout the centuries, poison has had a very special place in English law. For a brief period in the 16th century, wilful poisoning was high treason ... a 19th century medical jurisprudence article assured its readers that the 'art of poisoning, in all ages of the world, has been chiefly indebted to the female sex for its scientific cultivation'. [Art II Medical Jurisprudence No II 'Poisons', *Quarterly Review* 2 (1829)] ... Just under half of the women indicted for petit treason whose cases I have found were executed for poisoning their victims. [Mary Troke, 'but sixteen years of age' was burned at Winchester in 1738 for poisoning her mistress.] The twenty-seven found (collected primarily from printed sources such as *The Gentleman's Magazine*, the *Annual Register* and the *Newgate Calendar*) include thirteen cases of women executed for petit-treason in which poison was found to have been the method of murder.

Mary Blandy, who was executed in 1752 for murdering her father in what was described as possibly the most famous poisoning case of the 18th century, confessed to mixing a 'love powder' with her father's gruel with the intention of making him look more favourably on her unsuitable lover. McGavigan comments that while the thought of a love powder may seem to be ludicrous today, 'love powders' or 'love drops' were advertised and sold in English markets. Another account of the death of a recipient of such a love powder was reported in 1738, following the administration of a large dose of cantharides in coffee. 'Clearly, lethal substances were available from sources other than apothecaries, and for well-intentioned and even useful purposes.'

In 1790 the practice of burning women as a penalty for some offences was abolished, but of those English legal cases examined by Shelley McGavigan and the trials mention on the internet, the only instance where witchcraft and poison are cited in the same breath is that of the unfortunate Joan Petersen. The French scandal of the *Chambre Ardent Affaire* probably fuelled the gossip of the time, but there is little evidence in law to suggest that witchcraft and poison were ever really the 'strange bed-fellows' they were claimed to be, despite popular belief and the familiar the use of deadly plants in wort-lore.

Magic: Witches Flying Ointment

There are more than 60 recipes for flying ointments – both ancient and modern – and the majority contain a base of rendered animal fat or lard and various herbal extracts, usually including *Solanaceous* herbs that contain the alkaloids atropine, hyoscyamine and scopolamine. There's even a vegetarian version using vegetable oil! The rather sketchy instructions for the preparation of these poisonous herbs vary so much that we could be forgiven for thinking as Samwise Gamgee in *The Lord of the Rings* suggests, *'you can boil 'em, bake 'em, mash 'em, put 'em in a stew'*, but the one thing that must always be at the forefront of anyone's mind is that all these herbs *are* poisonous when ingested. When applied to the skin, the alkaloids are absorbed more slowly into the body, although even applying to an open wound could have fatal results.

Flying ointments are a magical aid, a tool for those with the gift – and meant to be a boost for visionary experiences according to *Veneficium: Magic, Witchcraft and the Poison Path,* and Christian Rätsch writing in *Witchcraft Medicine*: '...despite the fact that none of the 'modern witches' themselves have any experience with the plants, they warn about the poisonous additives... It is considered trendy to brew 'modern flying ointments', guaranteed to not be poisonous. The recipes are nothing more than ineffective rubbish.' I'm with artist and herbalist Sarah Anne Lawless on this one, having seen many of the cavalier approaches to making flying ointment that advocate tossing handfuls of poisonous herbs about like a chef would throw in a handful of basil or parsley! Make no bones about it, if the ointment contains non-toxic properties it ain't gonna work; and if you want to blunder about guessing the right blend and dosage using the genuine toxic ingredients, you could land up in hospital or the morgue. **You have been warned!**

Chapter Two

The Proving Tree

The simplest method of using poison, according to the 12th century physician Moses Maimonides, was to add a single or compound poison to a highly spiced and/or chopped meal or in a victim's glass of wine; the rather logical assumption is that the strong flavours and uneven texture would mask the bitter taste and consistency of the poison. The heavy burden of preventing poisoning appears to have been spread among a veritable platoon of servants, from the head cook to the lowliest server, each with the responsibility for specific and often repeated steps for ensuring their liege lord did not succumb to a poisoning attempt.

In *The Art of Cookery in the Middle Ages*, Terence Scully describes a lengthy process for ensuring the food that reached the master's table was not likely to kill him:

> Everything that was intended for the prince's mouth became subject normally to two general sorts of tests, called assays: on the one hand, a test by means of a unicorn horn, and on the other, a test by what vulgarly we might today call guinea-pig experimentation. This second sort of test needs no long explanation: it derived from the principle that one should oneself be willing to stand the salubrity of what one offers to others while making the claim that it is perfectly harmless ... Clearly the test assumed that any poison effective enough to do in the prince – merely harming him could very readily prove in short order to be fatal to the poisoner instead! – would become manifest quickly and plainly enough to spare the prince the danger of ingesting it.

From *Riches of the Earth*, we learn that during the Middle Ages, through the Renaissance and right up to the French Revolution, the royal banqueting tables displayed a curious item of tableware – the Proving Tree. This was a metal stand (often attached to the salt dish) that had from five to fifteen different 'stone' pendants hanging from its branches. These stones were believed to detect or neutralise poison in any of the foods or wines served during a meal, and it was the chamberlain's job to dip the stones, one by one, into the food and wine as it was brought from the kitchen. Supposedly, the stones would sweat, change colour, or exhibit other reactions if poison were present – and it might be a long time to wait before his lordship actually managed to eat his dinner!

Although proving trees were hung with precious stones (sapphires, rubies and emeralds), they also sported flints, agates, shark's teeth, toadstones (or borax), and bezoars. The toadstone was usually a piece of fossilised rock honeycombed with cavities that had been filled with deposits of carbonate of lime, although in medieval times such stones were believed to be hidden in the heads of toads, hence the name. Bezoars were composed of lime and magnesium, but were not formed in the earth but as a concretion in the intestinal tracts of oriental deer and goats!

Another precaution was the application of a unicorn's horn (actually the horn of a narwhal) to the food or drink since it was believed that knives carved from unicorn horns would sweat, change colour, and shake in the presence of poison. The Greek physician and imaginative historian Ctesias of Cnidus (5th century) wrote: *'Those who drink from these [unicorn] horns, made into drinking vessels, ... are immune even to poisons if, either before or after swallowing such, they drink water, wine, or anything from these beakers.'*

Terence Scully also describes in detail how the master washed his hands in a basin of water that was tested twice by the unicorn horn, and how even the towel used to dry his hands was tested for poisons. Included on the multiple-step testing process were the pantry porter, the first master of the household, the first chamberlain, and the saucer, as well as several pages and serving valets. Each of the serving dishes was tested, as well as samples of the food placed on or in them. This included the trencher breads at the beginning of feast and the box of *dragees* (candied seeds) at the end of the meal. This complex sequence of testing, or some variant of it, was deemed absolutely necessary to ensure the welfare of any noble in the late Middle Ages. Ultimately, the principle was one of accountability: those who prepared and served the food were responsible for their lord remaining hail and hearty – on pain of death.

Using crystals and gemstones to detect poison was the chief use of precious stones in the precarious days of the Middle Ages and early Renaissance, and the use of 'touches' or 'proofs' survived well into the 17th century. The wearing of certain jewels and amulets was also believed to guard against poisoning, such as the image of a ram (or bearded man) carved on a sapphire had 'the power to cure and free from poison ...' while a lion or an archer carved on jasper gave help against poison. The image of a scorpion engraved on a bezoar stone when the moon was in Scorpio would also protect against poison.

Corundum or clear rock crystal and coral inscribed with the name of Hecate were also believed to protect the wearer against poisoning, as was Cretan agate and turquoise (*turquemal*). Amiantos (soapstone) was said to resist all poisoning, especially by magicians and borax or Lapis Bufon (toadstone) was the remedy of all sorts of toxins – *'iff a man hath taken Poysen Lett him swallow presently this stone and it being swallowed itt compasseth the guts and so expelleth the poysen ...'* Or a victim of poisoning could be cured by the application of the wondrous bezoar stone – a medicament much used in the16th century.

King John suspected the pears to have been poisoned *'by reason that such precious stones as he had about him cast forth a certain sweat, as it were bewraeing poison.'* One of the most popular was known as *langues de serpent*, which were possibly fossils or pre-historic arrowheads. Inventories of jewels from Edward I and Edward III include those that appear to have been worn as pendants. From the 14th century, however, they were more usually mounted, either separately or as part of a standing salt, to be upon the table ready for use. Henry VII in 1504 had a 'unicorn' bone and a serpent's tongue *'hang be a cheyne'* and the 1586 inventory of the plate of Mary Queen of Scots included a jewel set with a segment of a unicorn's horn.

The French and Burgundian inventories of this century also record a number of such *languiers*. The inventory of Queen Clemence drawn up in 1328 details a *langues*, and a similar jewel, fastened on to a silver-gilt base resting on four flying serpents was recorded among the treasures of the Duc du Berry in 1416. The inventories of the Duc de Anjou (1360) and Charles V (1380) also recorded several pieces of table-plate to which stones used to detect poison were attached.

Special tableware was often employed, such as goblets of Venetian glass, which popular belief said would explode if filled with poisoned liquid. The more wealthy might have eaten off plates and bowls coated with or made from some mysterious substance that would react to poison by changing colour. The Mughal Emperor Shah Jahan had a unique way of testing whether the food served to him had been laced with poison. He did this with a plate called the Zehar Parakh Rakabi (poison-testing plate) – an inventive utensil that was known to changed its colour when poisoned food was put in it, and if it could not, it would have broken into pieces on its own.

Stuff of the *Arabian Nights*, we might scoff but not so ... visitors to the Salar Jung Museum take pleasure in viewing the Chinese ceramics called Celadons. Consisting mostly of bowls, plates and vases, these smooth jade-like glazed pieces of tableware have 'simple but dignified shapes and designs added in a variety of ways', but another reason for their popularity was that they had the property of detecting food poisoning!

Celadon is a hard, dense, porcelain-like stoneware containing 'kaolin', one of the two elements of porcelain, but while the body of porcelain is white, the body of Celadon is reddish brown and the glaze is the most endearing part of Celadon ware. The manufacture of Celadon started in China during the Sung period (960AD-1279 AD) and the utensils quickly found their way to different parts of the world. The poison detecting potentiality of Celadon dishes (although it has no scientific basis) was a popular belief in ancient China and Sumatra, and later in Middle Eastern countries, that Celadons contain the quality of splitting or breaking when they came into contact with poisoned food.

If a guest didn't have special feast gear, he might have had a special ring that contained a gemstone, bezoar, or toadstone. By waving this over the food or dipping it into his drink, it was believed to neutralise any lurking poisons. Emeralds and amethysts were ascribed magical powers and besides using rings set with such gemstones, the nobility would also grind them into a powder and add this to their food. Larger gemstones were carved into drinking cups and used to combat poisoned beverages, according to E S Rodhe's *The Old English Herbals*. The gallstones and hairballs from animals' digestive tracts were also ground, set in rings, or simply placed in a goblet by the same reasoning.

These methods were obviously restricted to the nobility, leaving the masses to find cheaper techniques. Much of these prevention methods were based on religious beliefs and folk myth, as Terence Scully observed. Dating from ancient Jewish and Saxon practices, amulets and talismans were used as protection against many things, not just poisons. The Druids supposedly used vervain for such purposes, while the Romans touted betony's abilities. The 16th century herbalist John Gerard described hanging garlands of pennyroyal over doorways as a form of protection and having children wear necklaces made of peony root beads. Although it is the first of the seven Shrub Trees (less important than the seven Chieftain Trees and seven Peasant Trees) of medieval Celtic lore, the wild strawberry tree's leaves and flowers were believed to be an antidote to poison and plague in the 17th century.

There were all sorts of ways to avoid being poisoned, but what happened if the prevention failed? How did a medieval physician treat poison victims? Just as today, the treatment for non-corrosive poisons was to vomit the poison as quickly as possible. Emetics such as asafetida, cabbage seed, and fig tree ashes were used, as were warm or oily items like milk, butter, or water steeped with emetic or soothing herbs (to settle the stomach lining). Gervase Markham's *Good Hus-Wife* listed several herbal emetic recommendations: *'If you would compel one to vomit, take half a spoonfull of stone-crop, and mixe it with three spoonfull of white wine, and give it to the party to drink, and it will make him vomit presently; but do this seldom, and to strong bodies, for otherwise it is dangerous.'*

Alternately, various herbal medicines were believed to counteract the poison or venom and certain herbs were commonly used to combat certain toxins: mulberry leaves boiled in vinegar to combat henbane, garlic for serpent's bites, frankincense for hemlock, etc. Others were believed to be panaceas to cure any poison, such as fennel seeds boiled in wine, mugwort, mallow, meadowsweet, lovage. Oddly enough, some extremely toxic plants (rue and mistletoe among them) were considered to be effective antidotes providing the correct amounts were administered!

Another traditional release from poisoning was the use of a 'witch-bottle' – a device for turning the poison or curse of a witch against the sender by boiling the urine of the victim in a bottle. Needless to say there were some spectacular explosions and the stench of boiled urine is not one that goes away very quickly! In a 19th century case a Londoner boiled a witch bottle over a fire and claimed to hear the voice of the witch who was tormenting him *'and that she Screimed out as if she were Murdered'*. Most cases weren't quite so dramatic though people did swear by the efficiency of the method.

As fascinating as this history of poisoning appears to be, the one thing that is absent from these scholarly records, is the weight of 'evidence' *not* pointing in the direction of witchcraft. Undoubtedly there were witches who supplied poisons, and no doubt there were probably more who excelled at the art, but non-inquisitional records lack the catalogue of lurid detail so beloved by the judges for whom poison = witch = veneficium. In the ancient world, hemlock, belladonna and wolfsbane were popular poisons, but from what we can see from history, arsenic appears to be the flavour of the Renaissance nobility.

Magical Protection

Not all forms of prevention were tangible objects. Prayer, whether Christian or pagan, was the way for the common man avoided death by poison. 'The feast day of St John the Evangelist (December 27) was associated with wine because a legend held that by blessing a goblet of wine that saint rendered the poison in it harmless.' [*The Art of Cooking in the Middle Ages,* Terence Scully] Chanted charms were believed to transfer the poison elsewhere, as in the following Cornish charm from Rodhe's *The Old English Herbals*:

Tetter, Tetter, thou hast nine brothers.
God bless the flesh and preserve the bone.
Perish thou, tetter, and be thou gone.
Tetter, tetter, thou hast eight brothers.

Professor Malcolm L Cameron, an authority on Anglo-Saxon medicine, mooted an interesting idea concerning the incantations that often accompanied the recipes (spells or charms) as they were being prepared. He points out that:

> In the absence of clocks, giving an incantation to be recited, generally thrice, would give some consistency to the preparation time. Though acknowledging that by making the incantations mysterious (some were in dialects which would not be known to ordinary Anglo-Saxons) the placebo effect could be enhanced by making the medicine 'magical' ... that many Anglo-Saxon remedies have some measure of scientific underpinning and must have developed as a result of careful observation of diseases and the potions used to try and effect cures. It may be that an incantation containing foreign words could not be rushed so their inclusion would add to the consistency of the recitation time.

Chapter Three

Poisonous Flora

The Medici family cultivated many species of poisonous plants in their gardens and after visiting the infamous Medici poison garden in Italy, the present Duchess of Northumberland became enthralled with the idea of creating a garden of plants at Alnwick Castle that could kill instead of heal. The original idea had been for an apothecary's garden, but the Italian trip changed all that. Another visit – this one to the archaeological site of the largest hospital in medieval Scotland, where the Duchess learned about soporific sponges soaked in henbane, opium and hemlock used to anesthetize amputees during 15th century surgeries – reinforced her interest in creating her garden of these lethal plants.

So the Duchess set about collecting poisonous plants for her envisioned Poison Garden. While selecting the hundred varieties that would eventually take root there, she had only one steadfast requirement: the plants had to tell a good story. 'What's extraordinary about the plants is that it's the most common ones that people don't know are killers,' the Duchess explained. 'Visitors are often surprised to learn that the laurel hedge, nearly ubiquitous in English gardens, can be highly toxic.' But some visitors have had experience with laurel's sinister side after loading up their cars with pruned laurel leaves to take to the dump, drivers have fallen asleep behind the wheel of their car from the toxic fumes the branches emit.

Because of the plants' dangerous qualities, visitors to the Poison Garden are prohibited from tasting, touching or even smelling any of them. Still, even with guidelines in place, visitors can fall victim to the plants. This past summer, seven people reportedly fainted from inhaling toxic fumes while walking through the garden. 'People think we're being overdramatic when we talk about [not smelling the plants], but I've seen the health and safety reports,' the Duchess concluded.

The huge popularity of the Alnwick Garden clearly demonstrates the public's fascination with poisonous plants and as John Robertson, former Warden of the Poison Garden, remarked, every garden is a poison garden. The plants in Alnwick's Poison Garden, with a very few exceptions, can be found in most domestic gardens, or in parks and the countryside – and we've lived with these plants for a very long time.

Here are some of the traditional witch's more familiar plants that can be found growing in the woods, fields and hedgerows that can cause all sorts of irritations, painful reactions and poisonings. It should also be borne in mind that many plants that have beneficial, medicinal qualities can also cause a reaction if taken incorrectly, or in excess. The scientific details have mainly been taken from or confirmed by the *RHS Encyclopaedia of Herbs and Their Uses* by Deni Brown.

Aaron's Rod or **Great Mullein** (*verbascum thapsus*)
A tall, plant with grey-green woolly leaves and dense yellow flowers common on sunny banks and wasteland: at country gatherings the whole stem was set alight and used as a torch. Although most of the plant is toxic, its benefits can outweigh the dangers, but if during preparation of the fresh plant, the hairy leaves come in contact with the skin it could cause an unpleasant irritation. The seeds of mullein contain rotenone, a potentially toxic substance that may cause adverse side effects if ingested, especially if the seeds are consumed on a regular basis. Ingesting rotenone might induce convulsions, diarrhoea, abdominal cramps or vomiting. Some of the side effects of mullein leaf related to respiratory system include difficulty inhaling, tightness in the chest, tightness of the throat and chest wall inflammation.

Magical propensities for bringing courage; aid divination; banishment (exorcism); maintaining health; love attraction; protection.

Bluebell *(hyacinthoides non-scripta)*

A native woodland plant that is potentially as dangerous as the foxglove since it contains glycosides called scillarens, which are similar to the glycosides in foxgloves. Like the snowdrop, the bulb can be mistaken for onions and eaten. Theoretically, it lowers the pulse rate and causes nausea, diarrhoea and vomiting and larger doses could cause cardiac arrhythmias, hypotension and electrolyte imbalance similar to the effects of digoxin in overdose. Folklore tells us that by wearing a wreath made of bluebell flowers, the wearer would be compelled to speak only the truth; the chemical that makes the plant poisonous was used in alchemy.

Magical propensities for speaking the truth; preventing nightmares; love spells; easing mourning.

Box *(buxus sempervirens)*

This evergreen shrub is, generally, thought of as purely decorative, but it once had an important role in keeping malevolent spirits from entering the house or, when used as a border, prevents theft of plants from the garden. Its qualities are reputedly comparable in effectiveness to quinine for treating malaria, but it is rarely used as a herb today on account of its toxicity. Box contains the alkaloid buxine, which causes nausea, vomiting and diarrhoea. The leaves are poisonous to humans, but its unpleasant odour and bitter taste tend to minimise its ingestion. Death may occur through respiratory failure. Contact can cause skin rashes and the clippings should be handled with care.

Magical propensities for aiding for those who work with animal magic and spirits; protection for pets and livestock.

Bracken (*pteridium*)

A genus of large, coarse ferns noted for their large, highly divided leaves. They are found on all continents except Antarctica and in all environments except deserts, though their typical habitat is moorland. The genus probably has the widest distribution of any fern in the world.

In such a common plant we tend to disregard its poisonous effects unless we have to look after livestock that might eat it. Bracken poisoning causes depression of bone-marrow activity, which leads to severe leukopenia – a form of white blood cell anaemia; thrombocytopenia – an abnormally low blood platelet count and hemorrhagic syndrome. The young fiddleheads, eaten by the Chinese, Korean and Japanese, are actually carcinogenic.

Some researchers suspect a link between consumption and higher stomach cancer rates; and that the carcinogenic compound in bracken, ptaquiloside, can leach from the plant into the water supply, which may explain an increase in the incidence of gastric and esophageal cancers in bracken-rich areas. Along with the DNA damage caused by ptaquiloside it is shown that chemicals in the fern can damage blood cells and can destroy Vitamin B1. This in turn causes beriberi, a disease normally linked to nutritional deficiency. In cattle, bracken poisoning can occur in both an acute and chronic form, acute poisoning being the most common. In pigs and horses bracken poisoning induces vitamin B deficiency. Poisoning usually occurs when there is a shortage of available grasses such as in drought or snowfalls.

Magical propensities for healing; rain magic; prophetic dreams. Place the root under the pillow and solutions to problems will appear in dreams. Also used for fertility and protection.

Broad-leafed Dock or Sorrel (*rumex obtusifolius*)

Best known as the antidote to nettle sting; it has been suggested that the dock is alkaline and counteracts the acidity of the nettle.

'Touch a nettle, get a dock', however, is one of those beliefs where very few people occupy the centre ground. Most people either believe dock works in seconds or that it is of absolutely no value. The toxic component is calcium oxalates and its needle-shaped crystals can irritate the skin, mouth, tongue, and throat, resulting in throat swelling, breathing difficulties, burning pain, and stomach upset. Oxalates are poisonous in excess, especially for those with a tendency to rheumatism, arthritis, gout, kidney stones and hyperacidity. They are also acidic, which may affect sensitive teeth. Regular ingestion in small amounts can lead to calcium deficiency and to the build-up of kidney stones if the calcium oxalate formed is not excreted. In the past, young leaves were picked as pot herbs and according to Culpeper were 'as wholesome a pot herb as any'.

Magical propensities for attracting success.

Bryony black and white (*bryonia dioica*)
This hedgerow climber is such a strong laxative that even in the 16th century its unrestrained medicinal use was not recommended. Those who bought bryony root, thinking it to be mandrake, may have been 'up all night' but not in the way they'd hoped! It contains a glycoside, variously called bryonin(e) or bryonidin, which is a dangerously strong purgative, and an alkaloid called bryonicine. There is little reason for anyone to ingest any of the plant in modern times, but its historic use as an alternative to mandrake must have had unexpected, but unrecorded, ill-effects, according to the Poison Garden website. As an example of how large the root grows, Culpeper wrote, in *The English Physician* (1663), that the Queen's chief surgeon had 'showed him a root weighing half a hundredweight and the size of a one year old child'. This vigorous root growth meant it could be used to produce a counterfeit mandrake root either by placing moulds around the growing plant or by digging it up, carving it to shape and reburying it. Bryony root can easily be made to look

like the magical plant and was sold as 'English mandrake' by 'mountebanks and charlatans' according to at least one contemporary writer.

Magical propensities for initiating massive change in oneself.

Buttercup (*ranunculus acris*)
The buttercup thrives in damp meadows and pastures, gaily displaying its glossy five-petalled flowers, which can be seen and admired by all. The plant does, however, possess a darker side to its apparently attractive nature. It is poisonous, and will cause blisters to appear on the skin should the foliage remain in contact with the flesh for any length of time. Such inflammations prove slow to heal. The buttercup's unpleasant actions are the result of a substance called protoanemonine, which is present in the plant's segmented, toothed leaves. The chemical has long been used (and misused) by physicians as a counter-irritant to direct pain from one area of the body to another. Culpeper, the famous Elizabethan herbalist, well knew its character when he described it as: 'this furious biting herb'. During his time the buttercup was used on plague victims: a poultice of crushed leaves and salt was applied to the diseased areas. Blistering caused by this noxious compound supposedly over-shadowed the plague sores and, through the belief that the greater the pain diminishes the lesser, it drove the plague away. In reality, the treatment was merely an unproductive way of increasing human misery.

Beggars used similar poultices of crushed buttercup leaves to inflict their own skin with harmful ulcers. The purpose of this seemingly ridiculous form of self-mutilation was to arouse pity and possibly a few pennies. The plant was, therefore rurally christened Lazarus, and beggar's weed. The plant produces protoanemonin, which is at its highest concentration at the flowering stage. It is quite unstable and drying of the plant leads to its polymerisation into a crystalline non-toxic anemonin.

Protoanemonin is formed from the glycoside ranunculin when the plant is crushed. This instability may explain why buttercups are not viewed with the same venom as common ragwort, when it comes to livestock deaths. Since the toxins rapidly degrade, there is little risk of harm if ranunculus species are included in conserved forage. Ingestion produces inflammation of the mouth followed by abdominal pain. Ulceration of the mouth and damage to the digestive system follow. Diarrhoea occurs and urine can be bloody. Convulsions precede death. Protoanemonin is volatile and can be given off when handling the plant leading to eye and nasal irritation.

Magical propensities for bringing happiness; love; prosperity; healing.

Cinquefoil or Silverweed (*potentilla anserine*)

The only common flower with silvery, pinnate leaves and tiny yellow flowers, the cinquefoil's distribution is widespread, and the plant is common in damp grassy areas, waste lands and sand dunes. The plant's rhizomatous root is thick and inappropriate to be used for food as it is extremely bitter and has low caloric value; it is, however, used in herbal medicine as an astringent because of its tannin content, which is unusually high for an herbaceous plant. Direct application of its strong tannins onto the skin can cause scarring. Despite it being a common ingredient in Renaissance poisons and witches' flying ointment, the plant has extremely low toxicity; while Culpeper claims 'this herb expels any venom or poison, or the plague, other contagious diseases, as pox, measles.' It 'even cures the 'French pox', he notes one writer, Andreas Valesius, to declare. In heraldry, the cinquefoil emblem signified strength, power, honour, and loyalty; depiction of the five-petalled flower appears as early as 1033 in France.

Magical propensities for aiding divination; attracting love; money; riches and wealth; protection; sexual potency; maintaining sleep.

Columbine (*aquilegia vulgaris*)

Found in woods, damp places and fens throughout England and Wales and, although it is poisonous, it is often found growing as a garden plant. This pretty, easy to grow, early flowering plant may have played a significant role in terminating unwanted pregnancies and wise women in the villages would use its alleged abortificant properties to provide a community service. The plant is a member of the poisonous Ranunculus family and all parts of the plant, including the seeds, are poisonous if ingested. It is said that the dried crushed seeds made into a dusting powder will kill lice very effectively; also that it is possible that inhaling the crushed seeds dust or otherwise absorbing oils from them may cause poisoning, or cause the symptoms of poisoning. Charles-Ernest Cornevin in *Poisonous Plants and the Poisonings They Cause* (1893) wrote that the plant contains aconitine, and this seems to be the basis of its poisonous reputation because there is no scientific evidence for toxicity. In traditional herbalism columbine was considered sacred to Venus and carrying a posy of it was said to arouse the affections of a loved one. Culpeper recommended it to ease the pains of childbirth. In modern herbal medicine it is used as an astringent and diuretic.

Magical propensities for building courage; attracting love.

Corn Cockle (*agrostemma githago*)

Once thought to be extinct in Britain, this very rare purple-pink flower originates from other parts of Europe and is believed to have been brought into England by Iron Age farmers. At one time, most fields would have been filled with the poisonous flower, but modern agricultural methods and weed-killers all but wiped it out; it was also a very common weed in the 19th century. Although every part of the plant is filled with glycoside githagin and agrostemnic acid that could lead to severe stomach pain, vomiting, diarrhoea, dizziness, weakness, slow breathing and, in extreme cases, even death, the plant was used for generations in folk medicine, and even receives a mention in Shakespeare's *Coriolanus*.

Magical propensities: None found.

Cuckoo Pint or **Lords and Ladies** (*arum maculatum*)
The cuckoo pint is found growing in woodlands and hedgerows; its poker-shaped flowers are surrounded by a green leaf-like hood with bright red and orange berries, which are poisonous. Though the clump of orange berries formed in the autumn shines out like a beacon in its natural, woodland habitat, their acrid taste and speedy irritation mean that large amounts are rarely ingested and serious harm is unusual. The berries can cause irritation to the mouth and throat if eaten, which can lead to swelling and pain, breathing problems and an upset stomach. The plant is said to be one of the most common causes of accidental plant poisoning based on attendance at hospital A&E departments though this may be because the irritation of the tongue and mouth is more likely to result in hospital attendance than a simple stomach upset from, say, eating a daffodil bulb thinking it to be an onion.

In *Theatrum Botanicum*, John Parkinson's 1629 herbal, there are two recipes for *arum maculatum*. In one, small pieces of the root are mixed with lettuce and endive; in the other, the dried root is powdered and sprinkled over meat. These recipes are recommended for the '*unbidden unwelcome guest to a man's table*' because '*it will so burne and pricke his mouthe that he shall not be able either to eate a bit more or scarce to speak for paine*'. In Dorset in the 1930s, young girls believed that if they touched the cuckoo pint they would become pregnant. This may follow from the reference is John Lyly's 1601 play *Loves Metamorphosis*, which says, '*They have eaten so much of wake robin, that they cannot sleep for love.*' since many of its common names derive from the appearance of the spathe and spadix and this association with female and male genitalia gives the plant a colourful history. The name cuckoo pint, which should be pronounced to rhyme with 'mint and not as in a pint of beer', came about following disapproval of the name 'priest's pint', which was itself a shortened form of the original 'priest's pintle', meaning penis, because the irreverent said that the spathe resembled the oversized ornate pulpits of the time that meant lowly parishioners could only see the randy priest's pintle (the spadix) sticking above the lectern.

Magical propensities for increasing sexuality. It is one of the cards in the Druid Plant Oracle and symbolises the 'Alchemical Marriage'.

Deadly Nightshade (*atropa belladonna*)

For many, this is the star of the poison plants; named for Atropos, one of the Three Fates, who held the shears with which she could cut the thread of life. It grows in scrub, woods, woodland margins and thickets with the dark purple flowers appearing in June to August and the black, shiny berries from August to November. Most people have heard of deadly nightshade even if they have never seen it growing in the wild; its combination of providing deadly poison and its use to beautify give it a romantic attraction that is hard to beat. Add to that the hallucinations it may also cause and its fascination is complete. The plant's very name, 'belladonna', comes from its use by Venetian women to make themselves 'beautiful ladies' by causing their pupils to dilate. Before the advent of modern anaesthetics, belladonna was applied to the skin as 'sorcerer's pomade' to make the patient unconscious before surgery.

Belladonna contains tropane alkaloids, notably hyoscine (also called scopolamine), hyoscyamine and atropine, with at least five other toxic components having been isolated.

The enticing berries are slightly sweet and symptoms may be slow to appear, but last for several days. They include dryness in the mouth, thirst, difficulty in swallowing and speaking, blurred vision from the dilated pupils, vomiting, excessive stimulation of the heart, drowsiness, slurred speech, hallucinations, confusion, disorientation, delirium, and agitation. Coma and convulsions often precede death. There is disagreement over what constitutes a fatal amount with cases cited of a small child eating half a berry and dying alongside a nine-year-old Danish boy who ate between 20 and 25 berries yet survived. [*Poisonous Plants*, John Robertson] Though the root is believed to have the highest concentration of the toxins, the berries are usually the cause of accidental poisoning because they look so tempting.

Magical propensities for inducing visions and aiding astral projection.

Dog's Mercury (*mercurialis perennis*)
In the spring, this is one of the first plants to break through the dark earth in damp, shady beech woods and river valley woodlands, since it prefers sites that have water running through them. There is nothing appealing about the appearance of the plant and a 'dog's' plant is a term for one with no medicinal uses; it may have obtained this name to contrast it with 'annual mercury', which was used in cleansing enemas. Although the whole plant is considered only mildly poisonous, particularly at the time of the fruit ripening, ingestion of large quantities can lead to kidney and liver damage: symptoms are loss of appetite, crooked position of the neck, apathy and reddish-blue discoloration of the urine. Containing methylamine, trimethylamine, saponins and a volatile oil, it is emetic and purgative leading to nausea, vomiting and diarrhoea. Larger doses cause lethargy, jaundice, painful urination, apparently by making the urine acid, and produce a coma before death.

Magical propensities for protection.

Elder (*sambucus nigra*)
A large shrub growing in woods, hedges and on wasteland, the

elderflower and the elderberry are extremely useful for drinks, and have beneficial effects on the symptoms of colds and flu. Known widely in country lore and witchcraft's wort-lore as 'Poor Man's Medicine Chest' for all its beneficial properties, care must, nevertheless, be taken as: 'The leaves, twigs, branches, seeds and roots contain a cyanide producing glycoside. Ingesting any of these parts in sufficient quantity can cause toxic build of cyanide in the body. In addition, the un-ripened berry, flowers and umbels contain a toxic alkaloid.' Due to the possibility of cyanide poisoning, children should be discouraged from making whistles, slingshots or other toys from elderberry wood. In addition, 'herbal teas' made with elderberry leaves (which contain cyanide inducing glycosides) should be treated with caution. [*Root and Branch,* Mélusine Draco]

Magical propensities for banishing (exorcism); protection; healing; prosperity; peace.

Foxglove (*digitalis spp*)

These stately pink flowers are a very common plant found in both the garden and the wild; with the potential to kill in quite small amounts, but also the source of medication that has saved thousands of lives since its discovery in 1775. Contains cardiac glycosides called digitoxin, digitalin, digitonin, digitalosmin, gitoxin and gitalonin; during digestion these produce aglycones and a sugar. The aglycones directly affect the heart muscles. It produces a slowing of the heart which, if maintained, usually produces a massive heart attack as the heart struggles to supply sufficient oxygen to the brain. The acceleration of the heart ahead of this sometimes leads to it being wrongly said to increase the heart rate. The raw plant material is, however, emetic and eating a large amount may produce vomiting thus expelling the cardiac poisons before they can do serious harm. It is said that the name 'foxglove' comes from the fairies giving the flowers to foxes to wear as gloves so as to leave no trace when raiding a hen house.

Magical propensities for protection. Assists in communion with the Underworld.

Giant Hogweed (*heracleum mantegazzianum*)

This plant was brought to the UK to beautify large gardens and can grow up to ten feet tall in the wild where it is usually found along footpaths, canal corridors and riverbanks. The plant contains furocoumarins (psoralens), which produce changes in the cell structure of the skin, reducing its protection against the effects of UV radiation. These can be released from the plant simply by brushing against it. Exposure to sunlight after contact causes severe skin rashes, blistering and burns, but the effects may not start until about 24 hours after contact. It may take several years for the skin to return to normal, during which time any renewed exposure to even quite dull daylight will produce new burns. In some cases, a permanent change in skin pigmentation occurs and scarring. If you touch a giant hogweed, cover the affected area, and immediately wash it with soap and water. The blisters heal very slowly and can develop into phytophotodermatitis, a type of skin rash that flares up in sunlight and blindness if sap gets into the eyes. [*Poisonous Plants*, John Robertson]

Whenever giant hogweed is being discussed there will always be those who claim that the case against the plant is over-stated and that many other plants are more dangerous. That point of view seems to be opposed to the findings of a study of 29 years of plant poisoning reports that made it the second most dangerous plant, with only deadly nightshade exceeding it. It is now a federally listed noxious weed in many states of America.

Magical propensities: None found.

Greater Celandine (*chelidonium majus*)

Found growing on hedge banks and roadsides in the spring, the plant is often used medicinally despite the fact that it is poisonous. The toxic substances are isoquinoline alkaloids and are most concentrated in the roots though harm most often comes from the bright yellow juice of the stem which causes nausea, though its bitter taste discourages ingestion. On the skin, the juice produces burning, which is why it has been used to remove warts. The yellow colour of the juice, matching the colour of bile, led to its use to treat liver disorders in accordance with the Doctrine of Signatures, but isoquinoline alkaloids cause liver damage.

Back in the day Gerard wrote: *'The juice of the herbe is good to sharpen the sight, for it cleanseth and consumeth away slimie things that cleave about the ball of the eye and hinder the sight and especially being boiled with honey in a brasen vessell, as Dioscorides teacheth.'* In recent years, however, medical research has identified ten cases of acute hepatitis induced by preparations of greater celandine, which are frequently prescribed to treat gastric and biliary disorders and therefore greater celandine has to be added to the list of herbs capable of inducing acute (cholestatic) hepatitis.

Magical propensities for lifting depression; promoting happiness; assisting in legal matters; protection.

Guelder Rose (*viburnum opulus*)

A native shrub found in damp hedges, woods and scrub, the fruits of the plant are poisonous when raw, but edible when cooked. The flowers are produced in early summer and pollinated by insects. The fruit is a cluster of bright red berries that are edible in small quantities with a very acidic taste; it can be used to make jelly. It is, however, very mildly toxic, and may cause vomiting or diarrhoea if eaten in large amounts. The term 'cramp bark' is related to the properties of the bark's ability to reduce muscle tightness most often associated with relieving women's menstrual (period) cramps. However, this was also used during pregnancy for cramps or pain and general muscle cramping.

Magical propensities for regeneration and renewal; changes;

new beginnings; homecoming.

Hemlock or **Poison Hemlock** (*conium maculatum*)
Hemlock is a tall, much branched and gracefully growing plant, with elegantly-cut foliage and white flowers. Country people very generally call by the name of hemlock many species of umbelliferous plants, but the poison hemlock may be distinguished by its slender growth, finely-divided smooth leaves and perfectly smooth stem, which is distinctively mottled with small irregular stains or spots of a port-wine colour and also covered with a white 'bloom' which is very easily rubbed off.

Hemlock is one of the most poisonous plants on the planet, containing alkaloids, chiefly coniine, which paralyse the respiratory nerves, so that the victim dies of suffocation before the heart stops beating. The medicinal uses of hemlock date back to the first century AD, when Dioscorides used it externally to treat herpes and erysipelas. Death by hemlock poisoning was the method of execution adopted in ancient Athens, its most famous victim being the philosopher Socrates in 399BC. Under Jewish law hemlock was also admonished to criminals who were about to be crucified or stoned to death, in order to deaden the pain.

Magical propensities for work involving astral travel and for purifying ritual swords and knives. The flowers are said to be used in spells to cause impotence, and the plant good for ritually paralyzing a situation.

Black Henbane (*hyoscyamus niger*)
A native plant usually found on disturbed ground and sandy places near the sea, henbane could be relied upon by any poisoner; Dr Crippen used it to murder his wife in 1910. It is so poisonous that even the smell of the flowers produces giddiness, but in some cultures it is used for ritual and recreational purposes due to its strong hallucinogenic properties. The plant contains tropane alkaloids called hyoscine (scopolamine),

hyoscyamine (L-atropine), and atropine (DL-hyoscyamine) that causes dry mouth, thirst, difficulty in swallowing and speaking, warm flushed skin, dilated pupils, blurred vision and photo-phobia, vomiting, urinary retention, tachycardia, pyrexia, drowsiness, slurred speech, hyperreflexia, auditory, visual or tactile hallucinations, confusion and disorientation, delirium, agitation and combative behaviour. In severe cases there may be hypertension, coma and convulsions. Most modern cases of poisoning, however, seem to result from its consumption as a hallucinogen.

Various ways to administer henbane to treat toothache have been used. In Anglo-Saxon England it was believed that worms in the teeth caused toothache. In fact, at that time, it was believed that worms were the cause of all ills. Anglo-Saxon folklore talks of a great battle with a giant worm that resulted in the worm being cut into nine pieces and the nine pieces becoming the nine 'flying venoms' that were believed to be the cause of all pain and illness. This belief led to charlatan medicine men administering henbane seeds in a bowl of hot water held close under the chin. Through sleight of hand they would introduce small pieces of lute string and claim that these were the dead worms thus demonstrating the efficacy of their 'magic' potion.

It is often said that henbane was the poison used to kill Hamlet's father in Act 1 Scene V. Different versions of the text call the poison 'hebenon' or 'hebona'. The text talks of *with juice of cursed hebenon'*, but goes on later to call it a *'leperous distilment'*. It is this description that leads some scholars to propose that the poison must have been an extract from wood rather than simple plant juice.

Magical propensities for attracting love and to bring rain. It is also a herb of the Underworld.

Holly (*ilex aquifolium*)
Its role as the male god of plant life means it has a mass of

folklore surrounding it, but holly is best known these days as a Midwinter/Yule decoration. A heavy crop of berries is said to be a sign of a hard winter to come, but this particular superstition is applied to many berry-bearing plants. In England it is grown close to the house to keep malevolent spirits away. In Ireland it is grown away from the house so as not to disturb the fairies who live in it, and grown by the Druids close to the home to lift winter melancholy. It keeps away lightning so alcohol vendors would set up their stalls under holly at markets – thus the association with pub names.

Containing saponins, the fruits and leaves contain ilicin, ilexanthin and ilicic acid and a tannin plus cyanogenic glycosides. The berries are poisonous, but a small dose has been used as a purgative. A large dose, of the order of 30 or so berries, can cause nausea, vomiting, diarrhoea and abdominal pain. On the plus side, a farmer, accompanied by his wife, an employee and his wife who corroborated the story, spoke of the time they bought in some calves that all had ringworm, which spread throughout the herd. 'A farmer friend suggested an old remedy: hang boughs of holly around their byre. Within three weeks the ringworm had cleared up. We didn't believe it and don't know how it could have worked, but we'd do the same again if ringworm struck.' [Poison Garden website]

Magical propensities for attracting luck; protection; material gain; physical revenge; dream magic.

Hound's Tongue (*cynoglossum officinale*)

Found in dry grassy places, especially near coasts, this is a plant with hairy, grey-green leaves; maroon flowers appear in the summer followed by fruits covered in fine hooked spines. The toxic components are pyrrolizidine alkaloids called cynoglossine, consolidine, echinatine and heliosupine. Prolonged ingestion of pyrrolizidine alkaloids leads to liver damage and eventual failure and the plant is more a threat to farm stock than humans. The smell of the plant resembles dogs' urine so travellers would put some in their shoes to ward off dogs as they walked along.

The 16th century book entitled *The Boke of Secretes of Albertus Magnus of the Vertues of Herbes, Stones and Certaine Beastes* says that hound's tongue attached to a dog's neck where he cannot reach it with his mouth will lead the dog to turn in circles until he falls down dead. The author insists that *'this has been proved in our tyme'*, although why one would wish to do this beggar's belief! Rabbits are supposed to be able to eat the plant without harm and, until myxomatosis reduced the rabbit population, they kept it in check. Since the liver damage it causes may be a long time in appearing it is by no means certain that it is completely harmless to rabbits! In the 16th century, the roasted root was used as a suppository to cure haemorrhoids; while the juice of the boiled leaves mixed with pigs' grease and used as an ointment, is said to prevent hair loss.

Magical propensities for fertility; snake charming; masculine attraction and aids psychic powers if worn. The 'tongue of dog' used in traditional magical potions.

Ivy (*hedera helix*)
A climbing or carpet-forming evergreen with dark green leaves, common in woods and hedges; all parts of common ivy, especially young leaves and berries are harmful if eaten and capable of causing severe skin problems. Contains saponins, digestion of which results in hydrolysis and production of toxic substances. Ingestion has emetic and purgative effects and is reported to cause laboured breathing, convulsions and coma.

Though not, generally, a key component of the 'soporific sponge' once used to achieve anaesthesia for the performance of surgery, ivy does feature in one of the earliest recorded recipes. The precise origin of the sponge recipe is impossible to determine, but one of the first published accounts is found in the *Antidotarium of Nicolaus Salernitanus*, by Nicholas of Salerno. This was printed in 1470, but would have to have been written in the 12th century if it was genuinely his work. In this recipe, the normally quoted formula of opium, henbane and hemlock is augmented with mulberry juice, mandrake, ivy and lettuce. A sponge would be soaked in the juice of these plants and then dried to be held in stock until required. Wetting the sponge and placing it over the patient's nose and mouth resulted in the inhalation of the narcotic fumes. It is said that sleep lasting up to 96 hours could be achieved so that the body had the opportunity to recover from the trauma of surgery as well as the patient being insensible during the procedure.

Magical propensities for determination; strength; optimism; spiritual growth; protection against wayward spirits and angry elementals; ensures success in business and all new endeavours.

Juniper (*juniperus communis*)

A native shrub of heaths, moors, chalk downs, birch and pinewoods; the flowers are tiny cones that ripen in the second year, from green to blue-black. Volatile oils, particularly alpha-pinene, myrcene and sabinene, which are monoterpenes, can be extracted from the plant. It is capable of causing gastrointestinal upset though there is disagreement about how serious this could be. It has also been shown to contain high levels of isocupressic acid, which is known to be an abortificant. It is believed to have been used for this purpose in humans in the past – hence, gin, which is flavoured with juniper, is referred to as 'Mother's Ruin'. The 16th century herbalist John Gerard said, '*a large dose will lead to gripings and gnawings in the stomach but without causing either constipation or diarrhoea*'.

The wood was burned in the fire on New Year's Day in the Scottish Highlands to purify the house and its occupants, and also burnt before summer; and close to a sick person to drive out the malady. This use, to drive out disease, probably originates in the Middle Ages. In the mid-14th century, Sir John Mandeville wrote a 'pest-tract' in which he describes the treatment for plague. Plague was believed to result from the victim absorbing 'corrupt vapours' and was also thought to have a strong astrological connection. Treatment involved avoiding exposure to the vapours by preventing bathing or any other action that would open the pores and confining the patient to a closed room in which juniper branches had been burnt in order to cleanse the air. [Poison Garden website]

Magical propensities for aiding divination; banishing (exorcism); promoting healing and health; attracting love; protection; preventing theft.

Larkspur (*delphinium*)

Generally considered to be a garden plant and much admired for its beauty when in flower, delphiniums can cause fatal poisonings. Quite closely related to the *Aconitum* genus, its principle alkaloid, delphinine, is similar to aconitine; it also contains diterpene alkaloids that are extremely poisonous. Ingestion leads to nausea, vomiting, abdominal pain, muscular spasms. If fatal, death is usually due to respiratory collapse or cardiac arrest similar to the effects of monkshood/wolfsbane.

Magical propensities for keeping away ghosts and unfriendly spirits.

Cherry Laurel (*prunus laurocerasus*)

A very poisonous sedative herb, the common cherry laurel is a variety that is mostly grown as a large, glossy-leafed evergreen hedge in gardens. The leaves and fruit pips contain cyanolipids that are capable of releasing cyanide and benzaldehyde, the latter having the characteristic almond smell associated with cyanide. Cyanogenic glycosides are present in the leaves and when chewed they becomes glucose, hydrogen cyanide (prussic acid), and benzaldehyde. Cyanide starves the central nervous system of oxygen and, thus, causes death. The plant has enough of the poison in the leaves to be used by entomologists as a way of killing insect specimens without physical damage, and there have been cases of cherry laurel leaves being taken to a tip by car and the driver being overcome by cyanide fumes given off by the foliage.

Confusing the two laurels and using the leaves of this plant by mistake instead of bay in cooking has resulted in poisoning; and if this occurs prompt treatment is essential. Graham Young, the 'St Albans' Poisoner' mostly used antimony and thallium but, when in Broadmoor for a time, he used laurel leaves to kill at least one person. His confession was ignored because, apparently, any death in Broadmoor produces a great number of 'confessions'!

Magical propensities for love and protection.

Lily of the Valley (*convallaria majalis*)
One of the most popular Victorian garden plants on account of its perfume, lily of the valley contains three glycosides; convallarin, convallamarin, and convallotoxin. Convallotoxin is one of the most active natural substances affecting the heart. It causes irregular, slow pulse rates and can cause heart failure. In addition, the plant contains saponins, which cause gastrointestinal poisoning. There was a superstition that anyone planting a bed of lily of the valley would be dead within 12 months. Gerard recommended it *'because it restores speech to those who have the 'dumb palsy' and is a treatment for gout. The flowers, put in a sealed glass jar and set in an anthill for a month, will yield a liquor which is an excellent ointment for treating gout.'*

Magical propensities for drawing peace and tranquillity; repels negativity; empowering happiness; mental powers. Use in magical workings to stop harassment.

Mandrake (*mandragora officinarum*)

A stemless perennial with a fleshy taproot and broadly ovate leaves; small white to blue-white, bell-shaped flowers are borne at ground level in spring, followed by aromatic yellow fruits. One of the most written about plants in history with whole books devoted to its properties and its ability to scream when pulled from the ground. It is a relative of deadly nightshade so contains the tropane alkaloids, notably hyoscine and atropine; the effects are hallucinogenic, narcotic, emetic and purgative similar to deadly nightshade and henbane. Mandrake root is supposed to look like the male form (having two legs, a body and often a hairy top) and, under the Doctrine of Signatures, its use *'would give a man that power which men are always willing to spend a lot of money to get!'* (see **Bryony**). Its high price was maintained, in part, by the difficulty of harvesting it.

Magical propensities for magical uses include protection; prosperity; fertility; exorcising evil. Carry to attract love. Wear to preserve health.

Mistletoe (*viscum album*)

An evergreen, parasitic shrub growing on apple, lime, poplar, maple, hawthorn and rowan trees; in spring inconspicuous yellow flowers are followed by poisonous, sticky white berries.

The Pharoadendron species contains a toxin called phoratoxin, which can cause blurred vision, nausea, abdominal pain, diarrhoea, blood pressure changes, and even death. The Viscum species of mistletoe contains a slightly different cocktail of chemicals, including the poisonous alkaloid tyramine, which produces essentially the same symptoms. Although mistletoe has therapeutic uses, eating any part of the plant (particularly the leaves or berries) or drinking a tea from the plant can result in sickness and possibly death. [HedgeDruid website]

Magical propensities for fertility; creativity; prevention of illness/misfortune; wear in an amulet to repel negativity and ill

will; protect against unwanted advances. Use to draw in customers, money and business.

Old Man's Beard or Traveller's Joy (*clematis vitalba*)

A native perennial found in hedgerows, wood edges and scrub, it may be a beautiful plant, but it was said to do the Devil's work for him by trailing into the other plants and choking them. Used medicinally in homeopathic preparations for rheumatism and skin eruptions, the plant contains protoanemonin and ingestion leads to severe abdominal pain and gastrointestinal irritation. Contact can cause skin irritation, which is why it was known as *herbe aux gueux* ('beggar's weed') in France, having once been used by beggars to irritate the skin in order to simulate sores. The acrid smell of the foliage causes profuse watering of the eyes and nose when inhaled.

Magical propensities: None found.

Pennyroyal (*menthe pulegium*)

A small member of the mint family, but less pleasant in aroma and containing the toxic compound pulegone that is notorious for causing abortion; for years the plant has been used for ridding the home of fleas. Two thousand years ago, pennyroyal was *the* herb used to terminate unwanted pregnancies. Dr Art Tucker, author of *The Big Book of Herbs* explains that pennyroyal induces abortions by first damaging the mother's liver: death sometimes follows. In modern times, most of the pennyroyal incidents involve the use of the plant's essential oil (generally used for therapeutic or homeopathic purposes or as an insect repellent), which is so potent that it should be considered a poison. **In the interest of safety, the advice should be *never* use pennyroyal essential oil for anything, not ever.**

Magical propensities for physical strength and endurance. Worn to bring success to business or to rid the home of negative thoughts against you. Carry when dealing with negative

vibrations of any kind.

Poplar (*populus nigra*)
Poplars are closely related to willow and similarly contain salicin, which reduces inflammation and relieves pain, but there do not appear to be any substances extracted from the tree that reveal why it was one of the major ingredients in witches' flying ointment. Most recipes contain leaves from the black poplar, or the use of the buds, which gave it its green colour, but give no hint why poplar was included among the other highly dangerous plants. Digging deep, the Wood Database mentions poplar in its list of 'wood allergies and toxicity' where it is said to be an irritant to eyes and lungs, causing blisters, asthma and bronchial problems, but that was the only reference to the tree's toxicity.

Magical propensities for evocation as well as banishment rituals. It is also strong with the elements of hope, rebirth, and divinations.

Privet (*ligustrum vulgare*)
A genus of about 50 species of deciduous and evergreen shrubs, privet has been recorded for medical use since 1000AD and in recent years it has been increasingly used to prevent bone marrow loss in cancer chemotherapy patients. Privet is a shrubby plant that bears elongated clusters of small white flowers and black berries. The plant can be found growing in the wild or in gardens. The berries contain chemicals (ligustrin, syringin and other glycosides), which can cause abdominal pain, nausea, vomiting, diarrhoea, headache, weakness, cold and clammy skin if eaten. The plant is considered to be very toxic and death can result if sufficient quantities are eaten by humans and animals.

Magical propensities make it useful for evocation as well as banishment rituals and divinations.

Ragwort (*senecio jacobaea*)

There are widely conflicting reports concerning the toxic qualities of ragwort, which is a very similar plant to tansy and contains pyrrolizidine alkaloids (PAs), which are hepatotoxic and can cause complete liver failure if ingested. There is no evidence that ragwort causes harm by contact or inhalation. In fact, there appears to be very little evidence of harm to humans resulting from ragwort except for those with pre-existing liver damage and a couple of cases where very young children were given large amounts of a herbal tea made with ragwort, which was said to be a cough medicine. It is used externally in the preparations of lotions to relieve arthritis, rheumatism, muscular pain and sciatica.

Misinformation about ragwort is very persistent and although there is no evidence of its harming healthy humans it may be more of a problem for horses. This is because living ragwort is extremely unpleasant to the taste and animals will ignore it if there is something else available. If it gets into hay, however, it has lost the taste but, being one of the few plants that retains its toxicity after cutting, it will poison horses fed on the hay if a large enough quantity is consumed. The symptoms it causes are described by the names given to its effects, 'Walking Disease' and 'Staggers'. It can cause blindness prior to death; death comes from liver failure, which results in the release of ammonia into the bloodstream which, in turn, destroys the brain.

Magical propensities for protection against evil influences. It can also be used as a ward against spells and charms.

Rue (*ruta graveolens*)

Commonly known as 'herb-of-grace', the plant is grown as an ornamental plant and as an herb throughout the world in gardens, especially for its bluish leaves, and sometimes for its tolerance of hot and dry soil conditions. It is also cultivated as a medicinal herb, as a condiment, and to a lesser extent as an insect repellent. The plant contains rutine, a glycoside, furocoumarins, alkaloids, tannin and essential oils; dermatitis due to photosensitization results from contact with the furocoumarins. There is some dispute as to how that contact can be achieved. There are those who say that simply being near a rue shrub may cause photosensitization, but most of the recorded incidents relate to rue being rubbed onto the skin causing the plant material to break down and release its furocoumarins. Gardeners say that the plant material must be damaged to release its ingredients since brushing a hand through a clump of the growing plant produces no ill effects – which accords with gardeners' experience of never wearing gloves when working with the plant. Scrunching up some leaves and rubbing them on a small area of the back of the hand, however, results in a slightly painful burn appearing a couple of days later after being exposed to sunlight. Ingestion causes vomiting, diarrhoea, epigastric pain, acute gastroenteritis hepatic and renal impairment; seizures may be observed and death can occur due to liver failure. In women, uterine haemorrhage and abortion may occur. [*Poisonous Plants*, John Robertson]

In folklore, it was used to keep various unpleasant things out of the home. It was hung in doors and windows to prevent evil spirits from entering the house and worn on the belt to keep witches away. Gerard wrote that, '*Burning rue will keep serpents away, this use being confirmed by the fact that a weasel will eat rue before it fights a serpent.*' Juice from a crushed stem spread on a wall around a doorway or window frame would keep fleas out of the house. **Warning: there are a number of internet sites offering repellent creams said to contain essence of rue and a few other sites even go so far as to suggest rubbing the plant itself onto children!**

Magical propensities for healing; health; mental powers; banishing (exorcism). Mix the dried herb in a bowl of spring water and sprinkle around a home to bring peaceful vibrations

or redirect a hex. **This plant is much more important in magic than in medicine.**

Snowdrop (*galanthus nivalis*)

Found in early spring in damp woodlands and hedgerows, the snowdrop is native to a large area of Europe and although it might be the harbinger of spring and everyone's favourite flower, the whole plant is poisonous, especially the bulbs. It contains two alkaloids, narcissine (lycorine) and galantamine as well as the glycoside scillaine (scillitoxin) and poisoning most often occurs when the bulbs are mistaken for onions. Initial symptoms are dizziness, stomach ache, nausea, vomiting and diarrhoea. Most people recover, but a fatal dose is said to result in trembling and convulsions prior to death. [Poison Garden website] It has been suggested that the mysterious magical herb *moly* that appears in Homer's *Odyssey* is actually snowdrop, and the substance galantamine, which, as an acetylcholinesterase inhibitor, could have acted as an antidote to Circe's poisons.

Magical propensities: None found apart from the above.

Spindle (*euonymus europaeus*)

Found in woods and scrub, this is a small shrub with insignificant small greenish flowers in May, but the crowning glory of the spindle tree is the profusion of bright pink, four-lobed berries that make it one of the most beautiful of autumn trees, despite its poisonous nature.

The poisonous components have not been fully defined although the effects suggest the presence of glycosides. All parts, especially the fruits and seeds, are harmful if eaten with symptoms appearing up to 12 hours after ingestion. The reaction involves diarrhoea, vomiting and stimulation of the heart; larger doses can cause hallucinations, loss of consciousness and symptoms similar to meningitis.

Magical propensities for inspiration.

Stinging Nettles (*urtica dioica*)
The lavish growth of stinging nettles is the sign of good soil although they are generally viewed as a troublesome weed; clumps are familiar sights in hedgerows, in field margins and waste ground. Its stem and leaves are covered in stinging hairs and as soon as the hair is gently touched, the brittle end breaks off and pierces the skin, injecting a poisonous fluid into the wound. This liquid contains histamine and other substances of undetermined composition, which cause severe irritation of the skin. The plant's dried leaves have been known to sting even after 200 years. It also has its domestic uses that can be traced back to the Bronze Age; young nettles provide a green vegetable in the early part of the year, but after June they become bitter and act as a laxative!

Magical propensities for banishing (exorcism); halting gossip; promoting healing; re-directing hexes; increasing lust; protection; managing stress.

Thorn Apple or **Angel's Trumpet** (*datura stramonium*)
All *daturas* are extremely poisonous, containing tropane alkalois similar to those in deadly nightshade and henbane that have caused poisoning and death in humans and other animals. The plants usually have an unpleasant taste so accidental poisoning from direct ingestion of plant material is unusual and most poisoning results from the consumption of a tea made from the seeds either for its alleged medicinal benefits, or for its hallucinogenic effects. A number of symptoms have been reported in 'herbals' going back to Dioscorides; with the overwhelming majority of reports saying confusion, delirium and hallucinations are the principal effects with drowsiness, sleep or coma generally following. Dilation of the pupils is such a common effect it gets mentioned in passing in some reports; agitation and convulsions requiring the use of restraints or sedatives are reported in around a third of the sources, a similar proportion give death as the

outcome of *datura* poisoning. [*Poisonous Plants*, John Robertson]

Only a few sources mention the muscle weakness that was supposed to make *datura* a useful murder weapon by rendering the victim helpless and cause memory loss, supposed to help whores get away with robbing their clients. The name derives from *dhat*, the Hindi word for these plants used as poison by the *thuggi*, bands of robbers and assassins in India.

Magical propensities for re-directing a hex; protection.

Tansy or **Bitter Buttons** (*tanacetum vulgare*)

Tansy was once a widely grown herb with a number of traditional medicinal uses, but one that has lost favour over time with the modern herbal community. Older herbals recommend the use of tansy for many purposes including as an anthelmintic to kill parasites: an infusion of tansy being given to children to kill worms. Tansy was also used to alleviate the pain of migraine headaches, neuralgia, rheumatism and gout, meteorism (distended stomach due to trapped gas), and loss of appetite. The danger with using tansy rests primarily with its thujone content, which is responsible for much of the plant's medicinal actions. Thujone is powerful, but toxic in large doses and the amount of thujone contained can vary from plant to plant making safe dosing problematic.

Tansy was also a popular strewing herb in times past because its clean, camphorous fragrance repelled flies and other pests. It is still a good custom to plant tansy outside the kitchen door and around the garden for the same reasons. Although tansy is useful as a vermifuge (a medicine that expels intestinal worms), and although it can be used externally as poultice to treat skin infections, '*it might be wise to look to less dangerous herbs that can serve the same purposes*'. [Annie's Remedy] Tansy was used to end an unwanted pregnancy by drinking a strong tea made of the leaves and flowers, which can cause miscarriage; and there have been reports of deaths in women attempting to use the tea as an abortifacient. Tansy essential oil is poisonous and should not be used under any circumstances. In large doses, tansy becomes a violent irritant, and induces venous congestion of the abdominal organs if taken internally since toxic metabolites are produced as the oil is broken down in the liver and digestive tract.

Magical propensities for maintaining health and longevity.

Umbelliferous Plants (*apiaceae* or *umbelliferae*)

Commonly known as the celery, carrot or parsley family, these are mostly aromatic plants with hollow stems. Included in this family are the well-known plants: angelica, anise, arracacia, asafoetida, caraway, carrot, celery, chervil, cicely, coriander (cilantro), culantro, cumin, dill, fennel, hemlock, lovage, cow parsley, parsley, parsnip, cow parsnip, sea holly, giant hogweed and silphium – a plant whose identity is unclear and which may be extinct.

The poisonous members of the *apiaceae* family have been used for a variety of purposes globally. The poisonous *oenanthe crocata* has been used to stupefy fish; *cicuta douglasii* has been used as an aid in suicides, and arrow poisons have been made from various other family species – all yielding just as potent a poison as in Socrates' day. One that needs to be given a wide berth is fool's parsley, *aethusa cynapium*, a diminutive plant that appears somewhat similar to a popular, tasty umbellifer: pignut, *conopodium majus*. A clue to the toxicity of fool's parsley is strongly indicated by some of its common names: dog poison, poison parsley and lesser hemlock.

Magical propensities: see individual plants.

Water Hemlock, Cowbane or Dropwort (*oenanthe crocata*)

Though somewhat similar in appearance to the poison hemlock, this perennial of marshy grounds and stream borders can kill much more quickly. So quickly, that, historically, it hasn't always been identified as the cause of sudden death. This plant is frequently described as 'probably the most poisonous plant found in Britain'. In 1987 it was said that there had been 14 reported cases in the 20th century, nine of which were fatal. In 1992 water dropwort growing wild (the foliage is similar to celery) did kill two foragers.

A peculiarity of the foliage is the venation pattern – the veins apparently ending within the notches instead of extending to the tips of the teeth. The small white flowers, appearing in summer, are borne at the branch end in compound, long-stalked umbels, after the manner of parsley blossoms. All parts of the plant are poisonous if eaten, producing nausea and convulsions, the fleshy, tuberous roots being especially harmful. The roots contain the greatest concentration, and it is sometimes said that the toxins are stronger in the winter, but this may be due to the absence of other vegetation in winter time. A small amount of raw plant material is fatal – causing nausea, convulsions, excessive salivation and dilated pupils. Death comes quickly. The roots have been eaten in mistake for parsnips and the stems have been eaten as celery. The smell of the plant causes giddiness and 17th century botanist Thomas Johnson was concerned that apothecaries did not know enough about plants to avoid being supplied with the wrong ones by the 'green women' who gathered and sold them. He implies that this mistaken supply may not, always, have been an innocent error on behalf of the gatherers. [Poison Garden website]

Magical propensities for protection and grounding; cursing; astral projection; banishing.

Wild daffodils (*narcissus spp*)

This abundant spring favourite appears to be one of the most frequent causes of accidental poisoning, but as the symptoms are not generally severe, treatment at home is the rule and incidents do not find their way into official statistics. All parts of the plant are poisonous: the bulb holds the largest concentration of toxins, but the flowers are mildly toxic, too. *'An extract of the bulb, when applied to open wounds, has caused staggering, numbness of the whole nervous system and paralysis of the heart,'* according to Margaret Grieve in *A Modern Herbal*. It contains two alkaloids, narcissine (lycorine) and galantamine as well as the glycoside scillaine (scillitoxin). Eating as little as half a bulb has been known to cause an unpleasant stomach upset lasting a couple of days but, typically, the symptoms are not so serious as to need hospital treatment.

Magical propensities for increasing fertility; love divination; attracting luck.

Wild Parsnip (*patinaca sativa*)
Reported incidents seem to refer to wild parsnips more often than the cultivated varieties, and some research suggests that fungal infection of the root results in a significant increase in the furocoumarin content and may explain why the problem occurs only with older plants. It may be, however, that bright sunlight is required to cause the burning to occur and thus parsnips harvested through the winter do not give rise to the problem of severe blistering. People who grow parsnips often leave them in the ground and harvest them as required. This may mean that, in the spring, unharvested plants run to seed and this is where the danger lies.

Magical propensities: None found.

Wolfsbane or **Monkshood** (*aconitum napullus*)
One of the most beautiful and also oldest and most deadliest of poisons. The principal alkaloids are aconite and aconitine; of these aconitine is thought to be the key toxin and one of the most toxic plant compounds known. Ingestion of even a small amount results in severe gastrointestinal upset, but it is the effect on the heart, where it causes slowing of the heart rate, which is often the cause of death. The poison may be administered by absorption

through broken skin or open wounds and there are reports of florists being unwell after working with the flowers. Its distinctive taste makes it unpleasant to eat so accidental poisoning is extremely rare but not unknown. The taste is described as initially very bitter followed by a burning sensation and, then, a numbing of the mouth. All parts of the plant are extremely poisonous if eaten and may cause systematic poisoning if handled.

Magical propensities for invisibility and protection from evil. Excellent for redirecting predators.

Woody Nightshade (*solanum dulcamara*)
A sprawling plant found in hedges, woodland and on waste ground with beautiful purple flowers. All parts of the plant, particularly the leaves and unripe berries, are toxic if eaten.

The red berries are very attractive, and very toxic, containing solanine, an alkaloid glycoside that increases bodily secretions and leads to vomiting and convulsions. The strength of its actions is said to be very dependent on the soil in which it grows with light, dry soils increasing its effects. Many books say that *dulcamara* means bitter sweet and comes from the taste of the berries being at first bitter but then very sweet. This view leads to its alternative English name, 'bittersweet'. Even modern books repeat the line that the taste is first bitter then sweet, but Gerard described the berries as being *'of a sweet taste at the first, but after very unpleasant, of a strong savour'*. Nevertheless, the berries of this plant have been revered for thousands of years and remains of them were found in the tomb of Tutankhamen, according to Lise Manniche in *An Ancient Egyptian Herbal*.

Magical propensities for adding power to any magic done on the Dark Moon; any variety of nightshade can be used to honour the dead or in rituals involving death and the spirit realm; balancing energy.

Black Nightshade (*solanum nigrum*)

A native annual of waste places, roadsides and a garden weed; in autumn it bears shiny black berries that are poisonous, particularly after a very sunny season. Poisoning symptoms are typically delayed for six to 12 hours after ingestion and the initial symptoms of toxicity include fever, sweating, vomiting, abdominal pain, diarrhoea, confusion, and drowsiness. Death from ingesting large amounts of the plant results from cardiac arrhythmias and respiratory failure. Black nightshade is highly variable, and the toxin levels may also be affected by the plant's growing conditions, with the toxins mostly concentrated in the unripe green berries, and immature fruit should be treated as poisonous. Most cases of suspected poisoning are due to consumption of leaves or unripe fruit. *Solanum nigrum* has been recorded from deposits of the Paleolithic and Mesolithic era of ancient Britain and it has been suggested that it was part of the native flora before Neolithic agriculture emerged. The species was mentioned by Pliny the Elder in the first century AD and by the great herbalists, including Dioscorides.

Magical propensities for use in lunar magic or works related to death; in witchcraft, it is a classic Samhain plant. Also, contrary to Grieves and Cunningham, black nightshade is *not* another name for henbane (see above).

Yew (*taxus baccata*)

A native tree still fairly common in the wild in England and Wales where it can live to a very great age, perhaps even some 3,000 years; it is an impressive evergreen that is rich in myths, legends and folklore. All parts of the tree are toxic to humans and animals with the exception of the yew berries (however, their *seeds* are toxic); ingestion and subsequent excretion by birds whose beaks and digestive systems do not break down the seeds' coating are the primary means of yew dispersal. Though the berries are harmless, the seed within is highly toxic. Unbroken it will pass through the body without being digested, but if the seed is chewed poisoning can occur with as few as three berries. Male and monoecious yews release cytotoxic pollen, which can cause headaches, lethargy, aching joints, itching, and skin rashes; it is also a trigger for asthma. The foliage itself remains toxic even when wilted, and toxicity increases in potency when dried. The major toxin within the yew is the alkaloid taxine. Symptoms of yew poisoning include an accelerated heart rate, muscle tremors, convulsions, collapse, difficulty breathing, circulation impairment and eventually cardiac arrest. However, there may be no symptoms, and if poisoning remains undetected death may occur within hours. Fatal poisoning in humans is very rare, usually occurring after consuming yew foliage, since the leaves are more toxic than the seed. Yew is one of the plants where the poison is not destroyed when the plant dies. Thus, branches removed from a yew by high winds or pruning will retain their poison. Yew is very long-lived and, in many cases, the yew tree in the churchyard predates the church so, the church was built round a yew tree because the pagan belief about the roots was so deep-seated. The roots of the yew are very fine and it was believed that if they grow through the eyes of the dead it will prevent them seeing their way back to the world of the living.

Magical propensities for raising the dead; protection against evil; immortality and re-directing hexes.

Deadly Fungi and Magic Mushrooms

There are some 3,000 species of wild fungi in the British Isles, of which about 50 are edible, but even if you don't fancy eating them, these strange variants provide interesting colour and texture to the autumn tapestry. There's lots of folklore pertaining to the identification of wild mushrooms from being able to peel edible ones, or poisonous ones turning blue when touched with a penny (a pre-decimal penny, that is), but the best advice of all is to leave well alone if you don't know what you're looking for.

Invest in a reliable guide and be safe rather than sorry: but even illustrations may often be misleading.

Since fungi were first used by humans, the poisonous nature of some of them has been recognised and exploited. The reason why some fungi are so dangerous is that unlike any other living thing, fungi are able to adapt extremely complicated organic compounds and their chemical make-up differs fundamentally from that of other flowering plants. One group of fungi assimilates poisonous substances that attack human organs such as the liver, kidneys and the blood circulation with potentially fatal consequences. The most dangerous of these fungal poisons are amanitin, orellanin, gyromitrin and muscarin. In addition to these poisons there are many fungi which, although they contain no dangerous poisonous substances, can cause gastric problems involving several days of sickness.

Nevertheless, people have been dying from fungi poisoning (accidentally or otherwise) since mushrooms have been gathered. The death-roll includes such notables as Pope Clement VII, the Emperor Diocletian and Emperor Karl VII; it is claimed that Euripides lost his entire family to fungi poisoning in one day and, according to Pliny, the Emperor Claudius was poisoned by his wife Agrippina, using mushrooms.

The effects of mushroom poisoning range from mild indigestion, cramp and nausea, to acute pain, loss of consciousness and ultimately – death. The incubation time usually varies from a few hours to some days – although one fungus native to Poland, the innocuous *cortinarius orellanus*, can take more than two weeks to show its lethal effect. According to *Mushrooms and Toadstool of Britain and Europe*, 'Because gastric problems often do not occur, and the kidney-damage is not always recognised as being caused by fungal poisoning, the source of the illness often remains undiscovered for a long time. Convalescence can take more than a year, and death can occur up to six months after the fungus is eaten.'

In Britain, the three most lethal are the **Death Cap** (*amanita phalloides*) found in deciduous woodland, mainly under oak and beech; developing a distinct sweet, honey smell when fresh or an unpleasant ammonia smell when old. The amanitin contained in the Death Cap causes the destruction of the liver and even small doses are fatal. The poison is active for years and cannot be destroyed by cooking – 50g of fresh mushroom is fatal to a human being. Or as one countryman said: 'Eat half a Death Cap and it's not a case of whether you may die, but how long it will take you to die.'

The **Destroying Angel** (*amanita virosa*) is found in coniferous forests at higher altitudes, also has a sweet, honey smell and contains the same poison as the Death Cap.

For many hundreds of years this highly toxic fungus, **Ergot** (*claviceps purpurea*), which finds a host in cereal crops, caused many thousands of deaths without anyone knowing of its existence. Ergot fungus contains a number of harmful substances collectively called the ergot alkaloids. Ingestion of *claviceps purpurea* has three principal effects; uterine contractions can lead to miscarriage; the blood supply to the extremities can be restricted leading to a burning pain in the hands and feet. This condition is one of those called 'St Anthony's Fire' and can lead to gangrene which, if untreated by amputation, may be fatal; a third of the ergot alkaloids is a close relative of LSD and is, therefore, strongly hallucinogenic. There is still a danger of ergot poisoning when 'organically grown' flour is used for home baking; these outbreaks seem to coincide with very wet summers as the fungus thrives in wet, warm conditions.

Ergot poisoning has been used to try to explain strange historic events, such as suggesting that the initial accusations of witchcraft made in Salem, Massachusetts, which became the subject of Arthur Miller's play *The Crucible*, were made by women suffering hallucinations after ingesting ergot. Mass hysteria then produced the full traumatic events. Ergot has also been offered as one possible explanation of the mystery of the *Mary Celeste* where the ship was supplied with contaminated wheat for the galley and the entire crew suffered ergot poisoning. Driven mad both by the ergot and the burning pain in their extremities they decided to jump into the sea to quell the flames of St Anthony's Fire. The 'Dancing Plague of Strasbourg' in 1518 is sometimes said to have resulted from ergot poisoning, but according to experts the symptoms displayed by the victims do not match any of those associated with the ergot alkaloids, other than the mental distress and mass hysteria.

With its red and white cap the **Fly Agaric** (*amanita muscaria*) must be the most distinctive of all the fungi. Frequently found in coniferous forests, mainly in pine plantations, growing in groups, this fungus is both toxic and hallucinogenic. Besides small amounts of muscarin, the Fly Agaric contains the agent muscimol, which causes disturbances of consciousness and hallucinations. Experimenting with this fungus is not advisable since it contains not yet fully analysed poisons that are dangerous to health and can prove fatal.

The elegant **Panther** (*amanita pantherina*) is found in both coniferous and deciduous woodland, but has no distinctive smell by which it can be identified. The highly effective poison acts like that of the Death Cap, but is stronger and can be fatal.

The **Yellow Stainer** (*agaricus xanthodermus*) found on forest fringes, in parks and meadows, looks very similar to its cousin, the common edible field mushroom (*agaricus campestris*). It has no distinctive scent, but smells unpleasantly of carbolic or ink when bruised. The Yellow Stainer should not be eaten as it causes violent vomiting immediately, although it does not permanently damage health.

A few species of fungi become more dangerous if eaten in conjunction with alcohol, for example: **Common Ink Cap** (*coprinus atramentarius*) can be found in gardens, waysides and in forests near inroads. Contains coprin, which is poisonous only in connection with alcohol; under no circumstances must any alcohol, in whatever form, be taken for 1-2 days before or after consumption. In true country-lore tradition, the common ink cap *is* edible – but it contains a chemical that reacts strongly with alcohol that can prove fatal.

Notes on Hallucinogens

Hallucinogens found in plants and mushrooms have been used for many centuries in spiritual practice worldwide and the actual cause of hallucinations is the chemical substances in the plants themselves. Unlike such drugs as barbiturates and amphetamines (which depress or speed up the central nervous system, respectively) hallucinogens are not physically addictive. Hallucinogens are natural and synthetic substances that, when ingested, significantly alter a person's state of consciousness. Hallucinogenic compounds often cause people to see (or think they see) random colours, patterns, events, and objects that do not exist; they sometimes have a different perception of time and space, hold imaginary conversations, believe they hear music and experience smells, tastes, and other sensations that are not real. The real danger of hallucinogens is not their toxicity (poison level), but their unpredictability. [*Pharmacognosy: Hallucinogens, Narcotics and Common Poisonous Plants*, Dr. Raman Dang]

Bittersweet Magic

Bittersweet, or woody nightshade, is probably the most useful 'poisonous' plant associated with witchcraft and very easy to grow in the smallest of gardens. This is a climbing or trailing shrub that can be trained along fences and trellises to form part of a 'wild' corner if grown with miniature comfrey, ferns and sorcerer's violet. It likes most soils and grows quickly from seed (usually spread by birds) and just needs thinning out in the spring. Since it is usually classed as a weed, small plants can often be found close to the mother shrub. With its purple-mauve flowers in the early summer and scarlet berries in the autumn, bittersweet can be an attractive addition to the garden if there are no children or pets to eat it.

Collected and hung in bunches, it protects the home and those who dwell within it (whether human or animal) from negative energies and misfortune. For its magic to work, however, no one else must ever know where it has been placed. It is also used for binding, enchantment, hexing, shape-shifting and transformation. A useful aid to the 'Law of Attraction' (not necessarily romantic) it can be used when working to create energy to draw like energy into your life, and in spells to balance energies and forces, light/dark, male/female, etc. Also useful in work to find a deeper connection with all things; release potential and discover true will. Surprisingly the magical action is very subtle and a wonderful plant to focus upon during meditation.

For all its beneficial properties, remember all parts of the plant are poisonous and hands should be thoroughly washed after handling any part of it.

Chapter Four

Cursing v Bottling

As we can see from the previous chapter, a large number of poisonous plants have beneficial uses in both domestic medicine and magic. Needless to say, when utilising a toxic plant in magic, we are adding certain extra deadly or potent energies into the mix and it is inadvisable to start messing about with deadly poisons unless we've made a thorough study of the subject – and not just by glancing at a paragraph in a book on herbal preparations!

Nevertheless, there comes a time in every witch's life when, for a number of justifiable reasons, an enemy requires dealing with and the traditional medieval methods open to the witch are not an option. Veneficium (i.e. murder by poisoning) carries a statutory prison sentence and, as Paul Huson reiterates in *Mastering Witchcraft*, 'The art of magical warfare (cursing and counter-cursing) is not one to be undertaken lightly.' To 'throw' a curse requires a tremendous amount of time, effort and focus and, as Huson explains, in order to make your curse into something more than an empty threat, a witch needs to build a dark current or vortex of power. Obviously it takes a long time to lay a successful curse and often may take several days before the witch has raised this dark energy by stoking up tightly controlled emotions in order to make the magic work.

As explained in *By Spellbook and Candle; Cursing, Hexing, Bottling and Binding*, curses, in the long term, are usually counter-productive and self-defeating, since few people who throw a curse bother to concern themselves with the far-reaching implica-tions, including the risk of it rebounding on the sender. Bottling gives a far greater 'control' over the outcome and if, at the end of the day, you decide it's really not worth the effort, then a bottling can be undone ... **a curse cannot.**

Many people confused cursing and bottling (or binding for short term) and, although similar in preparation, the long-term outcome is often employed for different purposes. Bottling lacks the finality or strength of a full-blown curse but, unlike the curse, *can* be 'undone' should it become necessary to negate the spell for whatever reason. Bottling is used long-term to contain both positive *and* negative energies; it is a method that can be traced back to ancient Egypt and the time limit is indefinite. It also lacks the risk of being returned to you, should your enemy realise what you are doing.

This WARNING must be borne in mind by any potential curse-thrower. No matter what the books may tell you about spells for lifting curses ... *there is no such thing*. Once sent, a curse cannot be lifted, called back, withdrawn or negated. It can, however, be deflected and, *if the cause is not just*, can rebound on the sender, especially if another magical practitioner is involved.

To bring about the desired (and usually unpleasant) results, as part of the bottling charm we will be utilising the harmful effects of certain poisonous plants to inflict vengeance on an enemy using 'sympathetic magic'. Both homoeopathic (the law of similarity) and contagious (the law of contact) magic can be conveniently placed under the heading of sympathetic magic. Both work on the principle of events being controlled from a distance by utilising an item to represent the recipient, or by arranging to place an item in close proximity to the victim. Both types of sympathetic magic can be used for positive or negative effect.

Positive magic says: 'Do this in order that so and so may happen,' while negative magic says: 'Do not do this, lest so and so may happen.' **The aim of positive magic is to produce a desired event**; the aim of negative magic is to avoid an undesirable one. Both consequences, however, the desirable and the undesirable, are brought about in accordance with the laws of similarity and contact.

Before proceeding, let us just pause for a moment to consider under what circumstances we, as individuals, would feel justified in carrying out an act of magical retribution. If our reasons are trite and petty, then it probably says more about us than it does about our intended victim. Over-reaction is a common reason that causes so much misery in the world, so the ability to administer a bit of on-the-spot self-analysis is worth all the guilt and agonising afterwards when it's too late, after all a witch is always taught to 'know thyself!'

For example: as the slogan on the T-shirt says: 'Believe in an after-life? Harm my dog and you'll know for sure!' Included in *By Spellbook & Candle*, this is an interesting adaptation of the Walter de la Mare poem and used in revenge for the killing (or deliberate injuring) of a pet dog, *The Gage* offers an example of an extremely powerful curse.

O mark me well!
For what my hound befell
You shall pay twenty-fold,
For every tooth
Of his, i'sooth,
Your life in pawn I'll hold.

But let us just pause for a moment and analyse the curse we are about to throw ... Here we are bringing down a curse that is *20 times* the number of teeth in the dog's mouth, which for an average healthy, adult dog is around 42. This means that the magical practitioner *must* weigh in the balance whether the punishment fits the crime. After all, it would be rather extreme if your neighbour had merely given your old mongrel a clout for attempting to ravish their prize-winning bitch! That said, this curse used against any act of cruelty against a dog – intentional or unintentional – might be seen to be justifiable. Cursing, like most areas of magic, is a question of personal responsibility and/or morality, but once thrown cannot be retracted.

And for the purpose of using poisonous plants to deal with someone who wishes or causes us ill, we'll stick to bottling for the purpose of this exercise ... and hopefully you'll see that it is a much more effective method for dealing with problems. Bottling also gives the sender a much greater degree of control over the situation since we are retaining the 'bottle' and can regularly give it a vicious shake, plunge it in boiling water, or stick it in the freezer if a 'reminder' needs to be sent to the offender.

The most effective container is one of those very small, brown chemist's bottles (either plastic or glass) that can be tightly sealed with candle wax. (There have been instances of eco-folk using fabric or leather pouches for bottling and curses and wondered why the working hadn't been successful!) Then there's the general ingredients consisting of rusty nails, bent pins, broken glass (ideally from old car windscreens) and broken razor blades. Keep a supply of these items in readiness – the natural and personal items (i.e. hair, nail clippings, saliva or a photograph/signature) are added for each individual working. Here are a few suggestions for dealing with day-to-day social 'unpleasantnesses' that we all encounter from time to time ...

Tell the Truth and Shame the Devil

... as my grandmother used to say. If finding ourselves in a situation where we are being seriously harmed by a colleague, neighbour or associate being less than economical with the truth then it might be a good idea to utilise the poison of the bluebell. Folklore tells us that by wearing a wreath made of bluebell flowers, the wearer would be compelled to speak only the truth; if the omission or lies are particularly damaging, perhaps the addition of buttercup sap to blister the guilty party's mouth.

Method: Make a small threaded chain of bluebell flowers and place around a photograph or piece of paper containing the signature of your enemy; fold and place inside a suitable container together with bent pins or, better still, fish hooks. Seal the container with white candle wax.

Spell: Taken from Shakespeare's *Henry IV, Part I*: '*By telling truth: tell truth and shame the devil. O, while you live, tell truth and shame the devil!* Keep in a place where it can be given a vigorous shaking from time to time and keep indefinitely.

To Stop Gossip and Slander

According to Culpeper, bittersweet '*is good to remove witchcraft both in men and beast, and all sudden diseases whatsoever*'. Magically, woody nightshade can be used for a 'Bittersweet Binding' against someone who is gossiping about you or slandering you. This binding is a method of 'staying a poisonous tongue' since woody nightshade is known to paralyse the central nervous system if taken internally.

Method: Here we use what is known as sympathetic magic, by binding the leaves or berries (both are toxic) of the plant, together with hair, nail clippings, saliva or a photograph of the guilty party inside a suitably sealed container. This preparation should be buried upright at the root of the woody nightshade shrub with the demand that its poison shall still the gossiping tongue of your enemy.

Spell: Adapted from the Bible: Psalm 140.3: '*Protect me from those who devise evil things in their hearts with the poison of a viper under their tongue.*' Stinging nettle can be used as a substitute, or as an addition required to 'sting' whenever the gossip or slander is being repeated.

The Quality of Mercy

Most legal matters require an antagonist and the more acrimonious the case, the more unpleasant it becomes, so a bottling in the early stages might just prevent a long, drawn out (and expensive) court battle. The yellow colour of the juice from the stems of the greater celandine, matching the colour of bile, is highly appropriate for legal matters.

Method: Place the stems of the greater celandine in a suitable container, together with a brief summary of the cases involved, together with the names of your enemy (the plaintiff or defendant) and urinate in the container.

Spell: *'All things by a law divine in one spirit meet and mingle.'* Seal with purple candle wax and keep until the legal issue has been resolved.

Halt!

There are often times when we feel it would be advisable to call a halt (permanent or temporarily) to a situation, either to prevent ourselves or someone close to us from hurtling towards disaster. Poison hemlock is ideal for ritually paralysing a situation until we can regain control.

Method: Take an inch long, hollowed out stem of the hemlock and place a rolled up photograph or signature inside, together with a single dressmaker's pin. Add hair or nail clippings, too, where possible and for greater control. If the working is to protect a friend, wrap a piece of fine ribbon around the hemlock stem and tie with a bow; if dealing with an enemy, use thin wire and twist the ends together with pliers.

Spell: *'Pinned by the sun between solstice and equinox, or until I release thee.'* Discharge the contents as soon as the danger is passed.

Petty and Spiteful

It's not uncommon to encounter someone's petty or spiteful behaviour towards pets or children and, providing no serious damage is done, a psychic slapping by using holly in a bottling might just do the trick: holly being the 'poison' used for protection and extracting physical revenge. Here we are working on the principle of events being controlled from a distance by utilising an item to represent your enemy, or by arranging to place an item in close proximity to them by using negative sympathetic magic, i.e.; 'Do not do this, lest so and so may happen.'

Method: Take a leaf from a male holly since this has the sharpest prickles and three berries from the female holly and place inside a suitable container, together with any personal items belonging to your enemy if possible; if not write the name and address on a clean piece of paper. A sprinkling of broken glass wouldn't go amiss either before urinating in the container.

Spell: *'Prick, cut, poison,'* (repeat three times). Each time your pet or (grand)child is upset by this person shake the container vigorously and repeat the spell three times to increase their discomfort.

Harassment

Personal harassment can take many forms on the domestic front – bullying at school or at work; noisy or disruptive neighbours who won't listen to reason. The legal definition is the act of systematic and/or continued unwanted and annoying actions of one party or a group, including threats and demands. The purposes may vary, including racial prejudice, personal malice, an attempt to force someone to quit a job, apply illegal pressure to collect a bill, or merely gain sadistic pleasure from making someone fearful or anxious. The traditional 'poison' in a witch's armoury to use to stop harassment is mandrake root, but this is not always easy to get hold of and the substitute is lily of the Valley. All parts of the plant are poisonous so make sure you wash your hands immediately after handling it.

Method: Dig up a small piece of root, grate it finely and separate into two piles. One pile mix with grated garlic (for protection); the other mix with soot. Place the LoV and garlic mixture into a small container, together with a piece of paper, folded three times, with the name of the person harassing you written on it and place in the bottom corner of the freezer.

Spell: *'Stay there and freeze for as long as I please.'* Fold the LoV and soot mixture into a folded sheet of kitchen roll and place where your harasser cannot avoid it ... or sprinkle where they walk ... since the purpose is to make sure the soot mixture clings to the fingers or shoes.

Sexual Harassment

Unwanted sexual advances are embarrassing and frightening because they stem from someone who finds you attractive, but won't take 'no' for an answer. Unwelcome sexual advances, requests for sexual favours, and other verbal or physical conduct of a sexual nature constitute sexual harassment and the key part of the legal definition is the use of the word *unwelcome*. Unwelcome or uninvited conduct or communication of a sexual nature are prohibited; victims may be coerced into going along with sexual talk or activities because of sheer embarrassment. Consent can be given to a relationship and then withdrawn when the relationship ends; once it is withdrawn, continued romantic or sexual words or actions are not protected by the past relationship and may be sexual harassment.

Method: Mistletoe is the poison of choice for dealing with unwanted advances and for this bottling you will need three mistletoe berries if in season (otherwise dried berries will suffice) and nine leaves from the plant, which should be placed in a suitable container, together with a picture, signature, written name of your enemy and any personal items you may be able to obtain. Now urinate in the container, seal with black candle wax and hide in the freezer.

Spell: *'Stay there and rot until time has forgot.'*

Garden Plant Theft

Now big business among the criminal fraternity, garden plant theft can be just as upsetting for the keen gardeners among us as a house break-in. A box hedge once had an important role when used as a border, since it was believed to prevent theft of plants from the garden; juniper has similar magical propensities and we use this spell to reveal the perpetrators.

Method: Make a list of the items that have been stolen from the garden; fold the paper into three and roll it into a cylinder small enough to fit inside the container. Take black cotton and wind it 13 times around the paper before knotting. Place in the container together with 13 leaves of pennyroyal or (not both) 13 leaves of juniper.

Spell: *'When the theft has fully acted been, then is the horror of the trespass seen.'* Place the container outside in the garden near where the items were stolen.

Family and/or Domestic Disputes

Families can cause us as much grief as enemies and sometimes it may be necessary to step in before a full-scale falling-out can develop. Pennyroyal rids the home of negative thoughts and can be used when dealing with negative vibrations of any kind.

Method: Take small pieces of paper and write the name of the feuding parties separately on each one. Roll into a cylinder with seven pennyroyal leaves divided between the pieces of paper, and tie using blue twine or cotton with only one wrap before knotting – and place in the container.

Spell: *'Once around, securely bound, now is the time for cooling down.'* Place in the freezer until all parties have sorted out their differences.

NB: When using containers for bottling, the watchword here is small is good. Often folk think the bigger the jar the more potent the spell, but this is not the case; the contents of a small 10ml pill bottle can pack just as big a wallop as a jam jar.

Magic: Releasing

Mark me well ... there may come a time when it becomes necessary to liberate your enemy from the bottle but, like the genii, it may not be possible to get him (or her) back in again. Remember we have used poisonous ingredients, albeit in small doses, and items that might prove injurious to wildlife if the contents are merely emptied away. When undoing a bottling (or binding) *all* the ingredients must be destroyed – and the best way to do this is by fire.

The gossip and slander may have stopped, the legal business resolved, the family nonsense sorted and your thief apprehended, so there is little point in retaining the spell. The simplest way is to burn the plastic container and let fire do the cleansing; if you used a glass container empty the contents onto the fire and boil the glass bottle to rid every trace of the spell. Sometimes we can empty the contents into fast flowing water, but not if there's broken glass, pins, rusty nails and razor blades in the mix. Remove any metal or glass from the ashes and put inside a container that is going to the tip and this will be disposed of safely and without any magical residue hanging around.

When it comes to harassment, however, these problems have a habit of hanging around and unless you are 100 per cent certain that the danger is passed, it might be advisable to leave the spell where it is – **indefinitely.**

Afterthought

All magic is dangerous, especially when coupled with poisonous plants and therefore it would be foolhardy for any beginner to think themselves capable of handling such powerful and unfamiliar energies merely on the strength of reading a book on the subject. Although the study and knowledge of poisonous plants is an integral part of witch-lore, it is important to fully understand what we are dealing with both magically and medicinally. Needless to say, 'leave well alone' is the watch-word when studying poisonous plants, and while learning to recognise them, a careful washing of the hands should be an automatic response if handling them.

And yet it should be evident that although there are considerable number of poisonous plants in the witch's store cupboard, every one of them has both medicinal as well as magic uses, in addition to their toxic qualities. In the old days it would have been a very unwise witch indeed who administered herbal healing but had not made sure the dosage was correct – because the newly emerging profession of physicians was waiting in the wings, ready to denounce them to the Inquisition if and when anything went wrong.

Poisonous herbs may well have been gathered to order by the 'green people' – men and women who had the right bestowed on them during the reign of Elizabeth I (The Wild Herb Act) to gather herbs and roots from wild, uncultivated land. It was an occupation that had been going strong since the late 14th century, but a new kind of medical herbalist had evolved – the apothecary – who purchased herbs collected from the countryside by these wandering herb collectors. In *Green Pharmacy*, Barbara Griggs records that during the 17th century herbs could also be bought direct from the herb-women in Newgate Market or Covent Garden.

Undoubtedly, witches used dangerous herbs for their inner rites to bring about altered states of consciousness, but this in itself is not evidence of *veneficium*. Witches also used a sinister form of 'short-hand' for the ingredients in their spells and potions, which in fact were ordinary plants. For example: 'tongue of dog' was hound's tongue fern, 'bat's ears' was holly, Jew's ear is an edible fungus, while 'dead men's bells' meant foxglove; similarly could 'fat of a new-born babe' simply refer to rendered animal fat of, say, a lamb or piglet?

Anyone, it seems, could acquire natural poisons on the pretext of needing its medicinal properties; the fallacy of witchcraft and *veneficium* being synonymous with each other points to a blend of fact, fiction and fabrication aimed at discrediting genuine practitioners of the Craft. In truth, long before the Romans came to Britain, traditional knowledge of healing plants was extensive; in Wales, medicine was a highly-regarded skill. The venerable traditions of the native priest-healers, from whom it is believed witchcraft descended, dated back to a thousand years before Christ.

So ... witches as history's poisoners? ... I think the jury's still out.

Sources & Bibliography

The Art of Cooking in the Middle Ages, Terence Scully (Boydell & Brewer)

The Curious Lore of Precious Stones, George Frederick Kunz (Dover)

Country Seasons, Philip Clucas (Windward)

The Encyclopaedia of Witchcraft and Demonology, Rossell Hope Robbins (Newnes)

Greek Fire, Poison Arrows and Scorpion Bombs: Biological and Chemical Warfare in the Ancient World, Adrienne Mayor (Overlook Press)

Green Pharmacy, Barbara Griggs (Hobhouse)

Herbs: Medicinal, Magical, Marvellous, Deborah J Martin (Moon Books)

Leedoms, Wortcunning and Starcraft of Early England, Vols I and II, Oswald Cockayne (London 1864)

Magical Jewels, Joan Evans (Dover)

Magic Crystals, Sacred Stones, Mélusine Draco (Axis Mundi)

Malleus Malificarum, ed Pennythorn Hughes (Folio)

Malleus Satani, Suzanne Ruthven (ignotus)

Man, Myth & Magic, ed Richard Cavendish (Marshall Cavendish)

Pharmacognosy, Dr R Dang (Al-Ameen College of Pharmacy

Poisonous Plants, John Robertson (BBC Earth)

RHS Encyclopaedia of Herbs, Deni Brown (D&K)

Riches of the Earth, Frank J Anderson (Windward)

The Roman Empresses, The Walpole Press (1889)

Root & Branch, Mélusine Draco and Paul Harriss (ignotus)

Veneficium: Magic, Witchcraft and the Poison Path, Daniel A Schulke (Three Hands)

Wild Flowers of Britain, Roger Phillips (Pan)

Moon Books

PAGANISM & SHAMANISM

What is Paganism? A religion, a spirituality, an alternative belief system, nature worship? You can find support for all these definitions (and many more) in dictionaries, encyclopaedias, and text books of religion, but subscribe to any one and the truth will evade you. Above all Paganism is a creative pursuit, an encounter with reality, an exploration of meaning and an expression of the soul. Druids, Heathens, Wiccans and others, all contribute their insights and literary riches to the Pagan tradition. Moon Books invites you to begin or to deepen your own encounter, right here, right now.
If you have enjoyed this book, why not tell other readers by posting a review on your preferred book site. Recent bestsellers from Moon Books are:

Journey to the Dark Goddess
How to Return to Your Soul
Jane Meredith
Discover the powerful secrets of the Dark Goddess and transform your depression, grief and pain into healing and integration.
Paperback: 978-1-84694-677-6 ebook: 978-1-78099-223-5

Shamanic Reiki
Expanded Ways of Working with Universal Life Force Energy
Llyn Roberts, Robert Levy
Shamanism and Reiki are each powerful ways of healing;
together, their power multiplies. *Shamanic Reiki* introduces
techniques to help healers and Reiki practitioners tap ancient
healing wisdom.
Paperback: 978-1-84694-037-8 ebook: 978-1-84694-650-9

Pagan Portals - The Awen Alone
Walking the Path of the Solitary Druid
Joanna van der Hoeven
An introductory guide for the solitary Druid, The Awen Alone
will accompany you as you explore, and seek out your own
place within the natural world.
Paperback: 978-1-78279-547-6 ebook: 978-1-78279-546-9

A Kitchen Witch's World of Magical Herbs & Plants
Rachel Patterson
A journey into the magical world of herbs and plants, filled with
magical uses, folklore, history and practical magic. By popular
writer, blogger and kitchen witch, Tansy Firedragon.
Paperback: 978-1-78279-621-3 ebook: 978-1-78279-620-6

Medicine for the Soul
The Complete Book of Shamanic Healing
Ross Heaven
All you will ever need to know about shamanic healing and
how to become your own shaman...
Paperback: 978-1-78099-419-2 ebook: 978-1-78099-420-8

Shaman Pathways - The Druid Shaman
Exploring the Celtic Otherworld
Danu Forest

A practical guide to Celtic shamanism with exercises and techniques as well as traditional lore for exploring the Celtic Otherworld.
Paperback: 978-1-78099-615-8 ebook: 978-1-78099-616-5

Traditional Witchcraft for the Woods and Forests
A Witch's Guide to the Woodland with Guided Meditations and Pathworking
Mélusine Draco
A Witch's guide to walking alone in the woods, with guided meditations and pathworking.
Paperback: 978-1-84694-803-9 ebook: 978-1-84694-804-6

Wild Earth, Wild Soul
A Manual for an Ecstatic Culture
Bill Pfeiffer
Imagine a nature-based culture so alive and so connected, spreading like wildfire. This book is the first flame...
Paperback: 978-1-78099-187-0 ebook: 978-1-78099-188-7

Naming the Goddess
Trevor Greenfield
Naming the Goddess is written by over eighty adherents and scholars of Goddess and Goddess Spirituality.
Paperback: 978-1-78279-476-9 ebook: 978-1-78279-475-2

Shapeshifting into Higher Consciousness
Heal and Transform Yourself and Our World with Ancient Shamanic and Modern Methods
Llyn Roberts
Ancient and modern methods that you can use every day to transform yourself and make a positive difference in the world.
Paperback: 978-1-84694-843-5 ebook: 978-1-84694-844-2

Readers of ebooks can buy or view any of these bestsellers by clicking on the live link in the title. Most titles are published in paperback and as an ebook. Paperbacks are available in traditional bookshops. Both print and ebook formats are available online.

Find more titles and sign up to our readers' newsletter at http://www.johnhuntpublishing.com/paganism. Follow us on Facebook at https://www.facebook.com/MoonBooks and Twitter at https://twitter.com/MoonBooksJHP